Call of the Camino

CAMINO DE SANTIAGO
EL CAMINO FRANCÉS

PARÍS

MAR CANTÁBRICO

TOURS
POTIERS
CHATEAULROUX
BOURGES
CLARITE
VEZELAY
NEVERS

LIMOGES
CHATEAUMEILLANT
LE PUY

BORDEAUX
PERIGUEUX

MONT DE MARSAN
CAHORS
ESPALION

ARZÚA
MELLID
PUERTOMARÍN
SARRIA
V. DEL BIERZO
PONFERRADA

ASTORGA

SANTIAGO DE
COMPOSTELA

LEÓN
SAHAGÚN
RONCESVALLES
VALCARLOS
ST. JEAN PIED
DE PORT

AUCH
MONTELIER
ARLES

OLORON
TOLOUSE

PAMPLONA
LEYRE

BURGOS
FROMISTA
VILLALBILLA
BELORADO
STO. DOMINGO
DE LA CALZADA
LOGROÑO
ESTELLA

MANSILLA
DE LAS MULAS
CARRIÓN DE
LOS CONDES
CASTROGÉRIZ
OLMASILLOS
DE SASAMÓN
S. MILLÁN DE
LA COGOLLA
NÁJERA
LOS ARCOS
PUENTE LA REINA
EUNATE
SANGUESA
JAVIER
JACA
VILLANUA
SOMPORT
CANFRANC

MAR MEDITERRÁNEO

Call of the Camino

Myths, Legends and Pilgrim Stories
on the Way to Santiago de Compostela

Robert Mullen

FINDHORN PRESS

© Robert Mullen 2010

The right of Robert Mullen to be identified as the author of this
work has been asserted by him in accordance with the Copyright,
Designs and Patents Act 1998.

Published in 2010 by Findhorn Press, Scotland

ISBN 978-1-84409-510-0

A CIP record for this title is available from the British Library.

Edited and typeset by Maggie Aldred
Front cover design by Thierry Bogliolo
Front cover photographs © John Brierley 2010
Printed in the European Union

2 3 4 5 6 7 8 18 17 16 15 14 13 12 11

Published by
Findhorn Press
117-121 High Street,
Forres IV36 1AB,
Scotland, UK

t +44(0)1309 690 582
f +44(0)131 777 2711
e info@findhornpress.com

www.findhornpress.com

For Mary,
who held the fort

✝

**Andate pur andate, non saran sparsi
i vostri passi in vano**

(Go, then, go; your steps will not
have been taken in vain)

Domenico Laffi

CONTENTS

PROLOGUE

For more than a thousand years pilgrims have been making their way on foot or horseback to the Spanish city of Santiago de Compostela, the purported resting place of the remains of Saint James, one of the disciples of Jesus Christ. While bicycles have for the most part come to replace horses, the majority of pilgrims still choose to walk the hundreds of miles which make up the "Camino," which in Spanish means a path, a road, a route, a way.

Pilgrims from every background are today drawn to the Camino from all over the world, and for a wide variety of reasons. What is nevertheless common to them all is that they will have left behind what is familiar, and habitual in order to wake each day to a new vista, to a new stretch of road, to the scents and the flavours of a land other than one's own.

Different viewpoints, different gazes. No two pilgrims, even of the same tradition, are likely to experience or to understand the Camino in exactly the same way. Some will have walked a hundred miles, some five hundred, some more than a thousand; some will be ill, some grieving, some confused, some celebrating; some walk out of devotion, or in fulfilment of a vow, others are simply curious. Different gazes, and ways of looking, different ways of seeing, even different ways of walking.

The Camino de Santiago is an ancient itinerary which has over the centuries attracted to itself numerous myths and legends. Before being established as a pilgrimage route to the shrine of a Christian saint, it was in all likelihood walked by earlier peoples, amongst them the Celts of north-western Spain, whose deity was the sun. Countless pilgrims have trodden this ground, ascended the same hills, crossed the same rivers, braved the same elements, sat down when the day's walk was done beneath the same stars, and listened to the same stories.

My own fascination with the Camino began with an interest in how it had been created and how it had flourished and evolved, reinventing itself in order to survive. As a writer of stories myself I was interested above all in the myths which had become attached, and which continue to be attached, to the Camino. From its invention up to and including its present-day existence, the claim that the Camino is more than simply a long distance footpath depends on accounts of its origin and history which stretch the credulity of historians.

A myth, according to the Roman historian Suetonius, is something that never happened, but always is. A myth is a truthful lie. Myths deal not with the facts of the world, but with our experience of those facts, tapping into strata of our psyche of which we are at best only partially conscious. Myths do not exist to be questioned: myths state what appears to those who accept their account to be obvious, but to those who reject the account, as risible.

The verification of a myth, on the other hand, is to be sought not in the world beyond, but within itself, in its power to persuade. Myths exist in order to persuade us of those things which we most want to know, giving meaning to what could not otherwise be explained. Myths can fill a gap and fulfil a need. Where a torch is lacking, we light the surrounding darkness with candles.

A pilgrim on the Camino is a pilgrim across time. Some conform more, some less, to what has been long since laid down. Some are open and outgoing right from the start, others keep their own counsel. There are many different ways to be a pilgrim, and each new pilgrim who sets out, and persists, adds one more way.

Those who have completed the Camino often report that, having set out with one purpose in mind, their eyes were subsequently opened to other possibilities and aspects of the pilgrimage, and many profess themselves to have been changed by the experience, both in their attitude to others and in their conception of themselves. It is claimed that such transformations can come about whether or not they were sought or anticipated.

Motives are seldom pure, nor do they come singly. Motives come in bundles. The more that I read about the Camino, the more curious I became. Once it had been the Apostle who was believed to work miracles on behalf of the pilgrim, and now it was the Camino itself. This I found intriguing, and the opportunity which the journey would present for looking into this matter further was one of the motives in my own bundle.

GETTING GOING

✝

Beginning is everything.

Spanish proverb

Certain birthdays concentrate the mind. For years I had been toying with the idea of walking one of the pilgrim routes to Santiago de Compostela, but it was not until I began my sixty-first year that it occured to me that the time for such an undertaking was at hand. Not only would it mark a milestone in my life, I would be engaged in a useful piece of research, and I would also be putting myself to the test.

"When have you ever walked that far before?" my wife argued. "And with a rucksack on your back?"

"Never," I admitted. "But I've never turned sixty before either."

"All the more reason why you should have more sense."

A number of different pilgrim routes could still be followed to Compostela, some commencing in the north of Europe and some within Spain itself. Within France, three of those routes converged at the foot of the Pyrenées to become, upon entering Spain, the Camino Francés, the best known and most travelled of the routes. Following the Camino Francés to Compostela from the small French town of Saint-Jean-Pied-de-Port, in the foothills of the mountains, would entail a walk of some five hundred miles, surely far enough for finding out what I wished to know.

I began to prepare. I joined a walking club in Edinburgh, the city in which I had for some time made my home, and took to traipsing up and down the far-flung hills of Scotland every weekend, regardless of the weather. I equipped myself with a compact sleeping bag, a top of the range rucksack, and a jacket "engineered for extreme wet weather." Never mind if the medieval pilgrim would have set off equipped with what was already to hand, I was prepared to sacrifice authenticity for comfort.

The Scottish winter dragged on. The weather maps of Spain that I called up on the Internet still showed snow flurries in the Pyrenées. While waiting I listened to language tapes, watched Almodóvar movies, and, instead of the *Scotsman*, began reading, from cover to cover, *El País*.

◆

No early documentary evidence exists to support the claim that James, brother of John, James the Greater, James the Apostle of Christ, ever proselytised in Spain, and yet, upon this claim, all else rests. The Apostle was also called "Bonarges", Son of Thunder, for his strong arms, his short temper, and the deep booming voice with which he was said to terrify the wicked and wake the sluggish. Nevertheless, according to later tradition, James made little headway in Spain, being opposed in his efforts by the indigenous Druid priests, men already skilled in protecting the crops and the livestock of the populace from harm, inasmuch as it was within human power to do so. So discouraged did the Apostle become that only a timely vision of the Virgin Mary rescued him from utter despair.

Historical evidence is lacking for the seventh century accounts of James having planted the first seeds of Christianity in Spain, but within a hundred years those first accounts were being further embellished. Having finally abandoned Spain and returned to Jerusalem with his few followers, James soon came up against the unconverted Jews living there and was brought before Herod, thus becoming the first of the Apostles to be martyred. Were this the end of the matter, the story that Spain would soon be constructing about itself would have lacked its hero, its warrior saint, its champion in the centuries-long conflict between Christian and Moor.

Legend has it that, although few in number, the disciples of James were devoted, so to preserve his corpse from mutilation they placed it in a marble sarcophagus, which miraculously, as in a dream, was transformed into a sailing vessel. Although rudderless, the vessel had as its pilot an angel of the Lord and as its destination the far distant coast of what is today Galicia. And there, (in the version presented by Gonzalo Torrente Ballester,) the holy body, having been taken ashore, was laid on a rock, which softened beneath the sacred remains, making a niche for it.

Thus the legend and the first miracle worked by the Apostle, after his death, in the lands of Galicia, and the surely somewhat shaky foundation upon which, in centuries to come, so much else would come to depend.

◆

By the end of March 2005 I could wait no longer. Spring in the Pyrenées, I decided, meant April. I had read that a fair proportion of those who set off from Saint-Jean-Pied-de-Port each morning gave up after the first day, so I was anxious to get that first day out of the way. I was also weary of being asked why I wanted to do a pilgrimage to the tomb of a saint when I wasn't in the least religious, a question for which I had no ready reply.

The cheapest way to reach the Middle Ages from Edinburgh was a budget flight to Biarritz. The day of my departure was grey and damp in Britain, and no better in France. Waiting at the airport bus stop in Biarritz was another individual with only a rucksack for luggage, a dentist from San Francisco who had walked the Camino the previous year and was back to do it again on account of how much he felt that he had missed. I smiled, being reminded of a Scottish friend who would read a book or see a film twice, once for the story and again for the symbolism.

Biarritz, with its Boulevard du Prince de Galles and its Avenue de la Reine Victoria appeared to be deserted. I had the Esplanade all to myself that evening, apart from an elderly woman walking her dog under an umbrella large enough for them both. The season had not yet begun, which explained the bargain that I had been offered on a hotel room.

In the old harbour I chanced upon a fish restaurant run by a Spaniard. The menu was chalked up on a blackboard, and I chose *rape*, having first consulted a small pocket dictionary and ascertained that this was the Spanish for monkfish. I was tempted, after consuming most of a bottle of wine, to reveal to the proprietor my plan to walk five hundred miles through his homeland, but good sense or superstition suggested that I wait to tell that story until I had walked at least the first twenty.

From Biarritz it was a short bus ride the following morning to Bayonne, from where a local train ran up into the foothills of the Pyrenées to Saint-Jean-Pied-de-Port. A wide assortment of pilgrims had already gathered at the station by the time I arrived and they were being entertained by an ancient individual with a bushy white beard and displaying an impressive assortment of pilgrim insignia pinned to his clothing.

"*Bonne chance,*" the old man kept repeating as he made his way along the platform, shaking the hands of the male pilgrims and kissing the cheeks of the females. "*Bonne chance, monsieur. Bonne chance, madame. Bonne chance, mademoiselle.*"

Once out of the city the small train ascended through a valley down which was flowing a river in full spate. My gaze met that of another pilgrim, a large Korean seated across the aisle from me. He smiled. His huge rucksack, which he had been unable to stuff into the rack above, was balanced on the seat beside him. His round face exuded good humour and confidence, but surely a rucksack that size was bound to take its toll.

We stepped off the train together, pausing on the platform of the tiny station to get our bearings. Park was his name, or rather one of his names, the one which non-Koreans found it easiest to pronounce. We made our way in the same direction as the other pilgrims, up the narrow Rue de la Citadelle to the *Accueil Pèlerin*. There, I had heard, we would be questioned as to our motives for making the pilgrimage, but Park, as a convert to Catholicism from Confucianism, wasn't worried.

"They can ask me anything, brother. Even a priest once said to me, 'Park, you're more Catholic than the Pope.'"

Neither of us was questioned. Our *credenciales*, the pilgrim passports which would from now on identify us, were stamped and we were assigned beds for the night in a small male-only dormitory. Already unpacking his saddlebags on the bunk above mine was a French Canadian pilgrim who knew the Camino well and who pointed out, on the list of refuges and their facilities which we had each been given, those which he considered to be most "genuine." There was the official version of what was what on the Camino, and there was also the grapevine.

I had to wait for Park, whose unpacking was slow and deliberate. In addition to what any ordinary pilgrim would have brought along, Park had a framed photograph of Pope John Paul, whose funeral would be taking place on the following day in Rome. Park polished the glass with a handkerchief before propping it against his pillow.

"That looks heavy," I said. "Did you bring one of your wife as well?"

"Somewhere," Park replied. "Also one of my children."

By the time we stepped back into the street the rain which had been threatening since the day before began to fall in earnest, sending us scurrying for the nearest restaurant. We ordered trout, which the proprietress told us had come out of the very river which ran through the town.

"Trout," Park pronounced. "*Truche. Trucha.*"

He had left no stone unturned. As well as studying the history of the Camino and carving his own *bordón*, or pilgrim staff, he had spent hours learning the rudiments of French as well as Spanish before leaving home.

"Brother," he continued to rehearse. "*Frère. Hermano.*"

Our bottle of wine arrived, followed by two huge trout. I watched as Park, with his large hands and thick fingers, deftly removed the backbones from them both. Was he a waiter back home? A fishmonger? Park then confessed that, back home in South Korea, he was a surgeon.

◆

The stones of Galicia were more accommodating than Lupa, the pagan queen of that still wild land. Asked by the companions of the saint for a plot of ground in which to bury his remains, the queen at once gave orders for the strangers to be imprisoned. Had they asked, or had they demanded? An angelic intervention ensued, the captives were released from their chains, and the soldiers who pursued the disciples of the Apostles suffered a similar fate to the Egyptians who pursued Moses and the Children of Israel across the Red Sea. They were swallowed up by a river.

A queen of Galicia would at that time have paid lip service to Zeus, but Rome was a long way off. Summoning her Druid magicians, Queen Lupa ordered them to conjure up a serpent of monstrous proportions and to place it in the path of the strangers. Shown a cross, however, the monster was cowed, lowered its head, and allowed the mariners to pass.

Approached for a second time, the queen appeared to give way. Not only could they bury their precious saint in the soil of Galicia, she would even give them a cart and a team of animals, but this, too, was a trick. The beasts she provided were not the placid oxen that she had promised, but four ferocious bulls.

"Let's see how they enjoy the ride," the queen said.

Once more, an evil plan was foiled. No sooner were the bulls shown the cross than they bowed their heads, accepting the yoke, becoming docile and biddable. The beasts themselves chose where the saint would have his repose: where they halted was where the sacred remains would lie.

The queen, discovering that the tomb was to be within her own palace, admitted defeat and was forced to concede that the marvellous symbol employed by the strangers was more powerful than any that her own magicians could wield. She gave up her own sepulchre for the saint's remains. To free the sacred precinct from the beliefs that had formerly prevailed there, an exorcism was performed and the Apostle was at last laid to rest. Afterwards, for the pieces of the story to add up, the whole business would need to be forgotten completely for nearly eight hundred years.

◆

I was awakened early by the sound of Park repacking his rucksack by the light of a small torch, repeating in reverse his ritual of the evening before.

In went the photos of his wife and children, and the Pope. From my sleeping bag I could hear that the rain was still pelting down outside.

Coffee and croissants were waiting for us in the kitchen, along with a weather forecast. Continued bad weather was expected, and poor visibility, and we were advised to avoid the higher pass and keep to the valley route. Park was nevertheless determined to stick to his original plan and attempt the more difficult mountain track.

"Don't worry, brother. God will look after me, God or an angel."

At the door of the refuge, before putting up our hoods, we shook hands and wished each other well. The exit from the town, appropriately enough, was through the Porte d'Espagne, after which yellow arrows painted on the pavement and on rocks would mark the turnings. It felt good to be underway at last, even if most of the twenty-seven kilometres that had to be walked that day would be uphill.

By the time I reached Valcarlos and the Spanish border, the rain had turned to sleet. The *venta* into which I ducked for a coffee was already crowded with lorry drivers putting away brandy, beer, and wine while they waited out the storm. These were the very individuals with whom I would be sharing the next stretch of the road.

Val-Carlos, Valley of Charlemagne. Thus was the landscape immortalized in the tenth century epic poem, *Chanson de Roland*:

> Huge are the hills and shadowy and high,
> deep in the vales the living streams run by.

The story goes that Roland, the nephew of the king, having fallen into an ambush, was too proud to summon help until too late, and so perished either at the hands of the Moorish enemy (following the courtly version), or was despatched (according to the historians) by renegade Basques. The sound of Roland's horn, the *olifant*, is said still to be heard by passing pilgrims, and a rock can be seen, by the imaginative, to be weeping bitter tears for what once transpired there.

After walking all morning without encountering another pilgrim, I began to get glimpses of a ghost-like figure in the gloom ahead. Only when I had caught up did I realize that, beneath what had turned out to be billowing plastic sheeting, there was a human being, a female pilgrim with a rucksack on her back. Simply by cutting a slit for her head, she had transformed the sheeting into a poncho.

Her name was Yvette. She spoke neither English nor Spanish.

"*Vous êtes*," I remarked, "*très chic*."

She replied, with a Gallic shrug, that people had to take her as they found her, and we fell into step. In the rain and wind and with her glasses as steamed up as my own, two sets of eyes were certainly better than one for spotting *les flèches jaunes*. Above us, when the clouds permitted a glimpse of the peaks, we could see that they were covered with fresh snow.

The last stretch of the climb was on a steep grassy track, and brought us out at the pass of Ibañeta. Only a short descent now remained before we reached the Augustinian monastery at Roncesvalles, which we could soon see spread out below us. The pilgrim hospital once run by the monks had famously welcomed *all* pilgrims, sick or healthy, Catholic or pagan, Jews, heretics, the idle and the vain.

Suddenly my companion's feet slid out from under her and she was left sitting on the muddy path, embarrassed, in a heap of plastic sheeting.

"*Merde!*" she cursed.

Seeing the look of fierce indignation on her face, I found it hard not to be amused. I asked her, in the best French that I could muster after such a tiring day, if she ate with that mouth.

"*Imbécile! Aidez-moi.*"

In the reception room of the monastery we found half a dozen wet and bedraggled individuals waiting on the benches without the strength to take another step. Anyone who had set out that morning from Saint-Jean-Pied-de-Port would by now have spent some eight hours on the road, more than enough of a day's work considering that many more such days were to follow.

No one there had run into Park on their way. Leaving my rucksack in the queue I went, with Yvette in tow, in search of the hamlet's single small bar. Among the clients drinking there was an English pilgrim called Lawrence, who said that he had seen no one all day. Nor would he have recognized a Korean, he added, if one had leapt out of the bushes and bitten him.

Yvette asked me to order her a cup of tea, which struck me as perverse. How difficult could it be for a French speaker to ask for a cup of tea in Spanish?

"So who is this oriental chap?" Lawrence asked. "A friend of yours?"

"I met him yesterday," I explained. "We had dinner together last night. He insisted on taking the mountain trail."

"And you are your brother's keeper, or some such nonsense?"

Lawrence ordered another beer, in English. An experienced pilgrim who had walked this way before, he passed on the useful information that pilgrim suppers at the bar had to be ordered and paid for in advance.

"Don't ask me why. People here make up the rules as they go along. Today there's one rule, tomorrow another. There's only one thing that never changes, and it's that everyone here does as he bloody well pleases."

There was only a single dormitory this time, with no segregation. The room was huge and contained a hundred or more double bunk beds, with each pair of adjacent bunks having been pushed together to save space. Yvette laid out her things above, Lawrence onto the mattress beside mine.

"You see what I mean? Once upon a time you couldn't even look at a woman in this country, and now it's one big free-for-all."

Park showed up just as it was getting dark, limping, suffering from blisters, but with the usual broad grin on his face. He hadn't been able to see much on the way, his boots weren't properly broken in, and he was carrying much too heavy a pack, but he would never have been able to forgive himself, he said, if he had taken the easier path. That, I supposed, was the difference between a Catholic and a Confucian.

Pilgrims were encouraged to attend evening mass in the monastery. As the final act of the service, those pilgrims who had arrived that day were summoned forward to the altar to be blessed by the priest. God was called upon to accompany and guide us, to be our shade in the heat, our light in the darkness. In the past, the monks would have washed our feet.

The monks would continue to pray for us on our journey, and we, in turn, once we reached Compostela, were asked to offer up a prayer for them. I found it difficult to believe in the efficacy of prayer, except as a device for concentrating the mind, but I did believe in reciprocity, and in the desirability of connecting the end to the beginning.

In the *comedor* of the bar the tables had already been laid with bread and wine. As we were taking our places an Australian woman, Sheila, asked if she could join us. She was an artist, she declared, and an energy worker.

"You repair power lines," I asked her, "after storms?"

"An energy worker performs healings," she corrected, "using energy drawn from the earth. I repair human beings."

A large tureen of soup was placed before us, at which point Yvette informed me that she was a strict vegetarian and that the mere sight of meat made her nauseous, so would I please find out from the waiter what ingredients the soup contained. I suggested that she check for herself, as the waiter was busy serving other tables.

"A vegetarian?" said Sheila. "She'll be lucky. She'd better learn the Spanish for 'egg and chips.'"

Park then asked if we had been able to make out the words of the vespers hymn. Park had certainly done his homework. The traditional psalm sung at a pilgrim mass, and so the one he had expected to hear, was: "He keeps my eyes from tears and my feet from stumbling."

"*Voilà!*"

On Yvette's fork, held up triumphantly for all to see, was a small piece of very fatty pork. It was perhaps wiser not to look too closely at the contents of the soup. Having deposited this unappetising morsel in an ashtray, Yvette asked me if, once the waiter had serving the other tables, I would be good enough to order her a salad followed by an omelette.

LEARNING THE ROPES

✝

As you follow the path, you also make it.

Confucius

Centuries passed during which the Apostle was allowed to rest in peace. The palace of Queen Lupa eventually crumbled and a forest called El Bosque de Libredón grew up over the tomb of the saint. Nowhere in the chronicles of the early Church is there any mention of Saint James having preached or been interred in Galicia, but much of Spain was by the ninth century in the hands of the Moors, and that residue of the peninsula which had remained Christian was in great disarray.

It is likely that the story linking James to Spain emanated from the monasteries of France, and it was a story waiting to be heard. The Muslims of the day had entered battle bearing an arm of their dead Prophet as a talisman, and had so far, on all fronts, emerged triumphant. The suggestion that James the Great, who was not just an apostle but also a close relation of Christ, watched over Spain, thus fell on fertile ground.

In Galicia, in the year 813, an unusually bright star was seen in the sky above the dense and mysterious forest of Libredón. Word reached Teodomiro, the bishop of the region, who ordered a path cleared into the forest. At the spot indicated by the star, excavations were made which revealed a tomb. No further proof was needed. Here, surely, the bishop proclaimed, lay James the Great, *Santiago Apóstol*, and work was soon underway on a chapel to house and protect the tomb and its sacred remains.

A bright light, celestial music, a sweet fragrance where one would have expected the stench of decay, a corpse still intact long after it had been buried, these were signs not to be ignored. The miraculously preserved remains of a saint spoke to believing Christians not of death and its corruption, but of the eternal life which they too had been promised would one day be their lot. So it was that for the faithful, in addition to the roads to Rome and Jerusalem, a third itinerary now beckoned.

◆

The lights in the huge dormitory, which had been switched off at precisely ten o'clock the night before, were switched back on at six the following morning. Some sixty half-awake pilgrims sat up, yawned, saw where they were, and began pulling on their trousers.

"Am I going blind," Lawrence the Englishman complained as we were rolling up our sleeping bags, "or is it still dark outside?"

Not only was it still dark, but there was a surprise in store when we looked outside. More than a foot of snow had fallen during the night, and it was still snowing heavily. Along with tea and biscuits provided by the two Dutch *hospitaleros*, there was a warning to keep to the road, as the paths through the forest would be impossible to follow.

"Be careful today. Walk in groups. *Buen Camino*."

Park had not yet begun to pack. He was sitting on the edge of his bunk, still in the underwear in which he had slept, staring down ruefully at his feet. We compared notes on the route for the day and once again wished each other well.

"Don't take any chances today," I added. "It's easy, in the snow, to get confused."

"That's why there are angels, brother."

Lawrence and Yvette were lacing up their boots. Paolo, a Portuguese pilgrim, asked if he could join us as he wasn't accustomed to walking in snow. Sheila, the Aussie, the one who repaired human beings, informed me that she was planning to continue on by bus.

"We're sure to meet up again somewhere further on," she predicted. "The Camino's like a caravan in the desert, people gather at certain oases where energy wells up to the surface."

Ours were the first tracks of the day. There was no wind and snow was drifting softly down. The road was narrow but easy to follow through the trees. However many decisions each of us might have made in order to reach this point, I said to Lawrence, which of us could have predicted either the enchantment of that morning or who we would have as our companions?

"Ah, so you're a philosopher," Lawrence said. "As you walk, you think deep thoughts."

"And you? You're the veteran, after all."

"Me? I walk in order *not* to think."

Seven kilometres from Roncesvalles lay the picturesque village of Espinal. Light was flooding out through the steamed up window of a bar, and already lined up on the counter inside were coffee cups waiting to be filled as well as portions of *tostadas* with butter and marmalade. A snowstorm in April was nothing unusual, the barman assured us, as freak blizzards were by no means uncommon there even in summer.

Lawrence sat down and bent over his coffee, warming his hands on the cup. Paolo sat waiting patiently, having asked for only a glass of water. Yvette, having freed herself from the folds of her plastic wrapping, asked me to ask the barman where the toilets were.

Paolo was struggling, not with the road but against the cold. He was shivering. He was dressed for Lisbon in the spring, not for the Pyrenées. The cheap plastic poncho which he had bought in the bar the night before was already torn and letting in the snow. Worse still he had hitchhiked from Portugal and had left his one warm sweater in someone's car.

"That's something that would only happen to a poor person," he complained.

By midday, Paolo was ready to give up. His wife had warned him that something like this would happen. The Camino, she said, was for rich people, not someone who could barely make ends meet in his own country.

"All the same," I suggested, "let's see if there isn't a remedy."

Yvette reluctantly allowed herself to be persuaded to sacrifice some of her voluminous plastic sheeting. She watched anxiously as I cut it in half. Lawrence dug a scarf out of his rucksack, and I fished out a flat cap. Paolo, by the time we had finished wrapping him up, and had strapped the bundle closed with a spare belt, appeared for all the world like some figure out of a Carnival procession.

"Two days on the Camino," Lawrence muttered as we walked on, "and two stray dogs. Where will it end?"

Coming into the town of Zubiri we crossed a bridge known as *el puente de la rabia*. Any animal that passed beneath the bridge, it was thought, would thereafter be immune to rabies. What was of more immediate interest was that the snow had by now turned to rain and just five kilometres more would bring us to that day's destination. A short stop at another bar, a round of *tintos,* and some generous slices of a freshly made *tortilla de patatas* not only filled our empty stomachs, but also raised our flagging spirits.

It was Yvette who noticed that Paolo had very little money, and offered to pay his share. Paolo, however, had produced some small change and was counting out what he owed. I smiled at Yvette, but shook my head.

"*Pas cette fois,*" I recommended. Not this time.

Yvette shrugged. She removed her glasses, which had become fogged, and wiped them on the tail of one of the several shirts that she was wearing. Despite the fuss that she had made earlier over surrendering any of her plastic "poncho," her heart was, after all, in the right place.

The *albergue*, the pilgrim refuge at Larrasoaña, was attached to the town hall. The dormitories were small, the showers were hot, and there were radiators on which to dry our socks. At the end of the village was a bar now filling with pilgrims, in sandals or trainers , still walking gingerly on account of blisters from having walked in sodden boots over tarmac.

Paolo, rather than join the rest of us at a table, sat down by himself at the bar to smoke a cigarette which he rolled for himself. He had no money for beer or wine and so refused to be invited by anyone else. His evening meals he planned to cook for himself in the refuge kitchens, or outdoors over a small fire lit beside the trail.

This was the same manner in which he himself had first made the pilgrimage, Lawrence recollected. No one, in those days, would have been invited to sleep in the town hall, what was then called a pilgrim refuge being no more than a shed full of tools or a barn full of animals.

"You washed in a spring or a stream. You cooked what you had brought with you. If there was a henhouse you helped yourself to a few eggs, and no one seemed to mind."

Park, when he appeared, did so in the company of an Irish pilgrim called Declan whom he had met on the road that day and who had helped him, Park related cheerfully, to climb out of a ditch after he had nearly been run down by a snowplough.

"True," said Declan. "The bastard never even noticed. Those fellows start off with a few drinks first thing when it's cold, and they keep themselves topped up all day."

There was steak on the *menú de peregrino* that night. We ate at a long wooden table and Yvette, rather than be nauseated by what everyone around her was eating, kept her head down and her eyes fixed on her omelette.

Wasn't she going to get bored, Park asked her, eating the same dish at every meal?

"*Probablement*," she replied stoically, without looking up.

◆

However otherworldly the life of a saint, whatever his trials or sacrifices, his goodness or the manner of his death, the relics which remained following his demise were, to those fortunate enough to obtain them, a commodity worth their weight in gold. A relic granted the protective power of the saint himself and was treasured by the royal houses of Christendom, as well as by its many churches and monasteries. What a coup then for an otherwise impoverished land, tucked away in a desolate corner of the world, to be able to boast of the remains of the only Apostle to be buried west of Rome.

A saint, by definition, linked the seen with the unseen through the miracles that he worked. No miracles, no saint. Any saint who ceased to work miracles ceased to be venerated, and might even be castigated.

A relic, a fragment of a dead saint, had the same power of mediation as the saint himself. A part was as good as a whole, and even a false relic, if believed in with unswerving faith, could bring about the mediation, the miracle, the outcome which, in the understanding of the day, admitted of no other explanation apart from divine intercession.

It was no small miracle that the body of Santiago should have turned up in Spain at all. The incredible manner of his arrival and interment and the subsequent discovery of his tomb in the wilds of Galicia were, for a people in need of a divine intercessor, of a *patrón misterioso*, the best proof that one had indeed appeared. At that moment, in the forest of that hitherto forsaken corner of Spain, history as it was conceived at the time walked hand in hand with hagiography.

◆

By morning, whatever snow had remained on the ground the evening before had melted, leaving behind only mud. Park, who had risen early in order to keep to his plan of reaching Pamplona in time for the midday Sunday mass at the cathedral, was nevertheless adamant that we must keep to the Camino this time and not attempt to avoid the difficulty.

"If God sends us trials," Park argued, "He does so for a reason."

"Does God *send* mud," I asked to pass the time, "or merely allow it?"

"Sometimes the one and sometimes the other, brother. That's why it's best not to take detours."

It was Yvette who paid the price for this. She was more than usually preoccupied that morning, which she blamed on not having slept well the night before, and so, by not watching where she was placing her feet, ended up in mud which rose well up over her boots and held her fast.

"Merde! Toujours la même chose!"

Her luck was always bad, she moaned. She attracted accidents. This was what had prevented her from ever learning to drive a car. It was easy enough to free her from the morass, not so easy to do so without laughing.

We found a stream in which she could rinse her boots and trouser legs, by which time a steady rain had once more begun to fall. Once more we put up our hoods and tightened the drawstrings.

"And what else do you suppose that God has in store for us today?" I asked Park.

"That's just what you can never know, brother. Only God can read God's mind."

We entered Pamplona, that city of Hemingway, San Fermín and the notorious running of the bulls, by walking over the ancient Puente de los Peregrinos, the Pilgrim Bridge. Here, in the city's cathedral, in a much-remarked act of conspicuous charity, the first dozen pilgrims to arrive each day were once fed, gratis, before the altar.

Dripping with water and splattered with mud we entered the cathedral, placing our rucksacks out of sight behind a pillar. Those arriving under umbrellas, and dressed to the nines, wanted to know where we were from.

"*Ah, Escocia, muy bien. Ah, Francia, muy bien. Ah, Corea, ¡qué maravilla!*"

Both Park and Yvette, when the time came, went forward to partake of the blood and flesh of Christ. Afterwards, as we were retrieving our rucksacks, an anxious verger approached us, not to reprimand us for the puddles we had left behind but to insist that we visit the cloisters, which were quite well-known.

We circled the cloisters, straining to understand the verger's explanations. The air was frigid and rain ran steadily down off the overhanging roof. Not for us the Pamplona of Hemingway.

We found our way from the cathedral to the Plaza de Castillo where, as it was a Sunday, the bars were competing for customers with elaborate displays of *pinchos*, various small snacks on skewers, the traditional prelude to that day's midday meal. Families here were still intact: the eldest members walked with sticks, the youngest cradling dolls or footballs. Now and again we could hear a whispered explanation for the three figures laden with wet rucksacks in their midst.

"*Peregrinos*."

Pilgrims.

Park, when he discovered that the *albergue* in Cizor Menor had a kitchen, announced that he would be preparing a noodle stir-fry for himself that evening, and for anyone else who might be interested. In his rucksack he was carrying not just the noodles but also two different sorts of soy sauce, brought all the way from home, and a jar of pickled vegetables. Also he had noticed some edible mushrooms growing just outside the village which he intended to go back and pick.

There was a rhythm to being a pilgrim. Having first washed ourselves, we then stood three abreast at the *lavadero* to wash out our soiled clothing, rinsing repeatedly until the rinse water ran clear. The biggest hardship which he had faced so far wasn't blisters or washing his clothes in cold water, Park expounded as we worked, but rather the food which was served to pilgrims in Spain.

"Pilgrims, I suppose," I suggested, "are generally hungry enough to eat whatever's placed before them."

"Not Korean pilgrims, *hermano*."

Only when he had tried out the stove, intending to brew himself a cup of tea, did Park realize that cooking a meal, even if only for himself, wasn't going to be as straightforward as he had imagined. Only one of the gas burners was working and that only on its lowest setting.

"You can't do a stir-fry on such a low heat," I pointed out. "Maybe a stew-fry…"

"Brother," said Park, deadpan, "I find your sense of humour highly entertaining."

I ventured up the hill to the local church, which was locked, so I walked a short way along the path upon which, come morning, we would leave the village, then sought out the bar which was offering a pilgrim supper. The *comedor* was not yet open because the cook had yet to return from his siesta, but I found Declan, the Irishman, waiting on a bar stool with a glass of beer and a bowl of crisps.

"I'm not a man for noodles," Declan explained. "As for vegetables, they're perfectly acceptable as a garnish."

We were already seated in the dining room, having been joined by Lawrence, when Yvette appeared, looking somewhat agitated. She had had a closer look at the mushrooms which Park had picked in the forest outside the village and she was sure that they were *toxiques*. I asked her if she had spoken to Park about the mushrooms, to which she replied that it wouldn't have done any good: Park wouldn't have understood her because his French was too bad.

"Did she say what I think she just said?" asked Declan.

"Isn't our oriental friend supposed to be some sort of doctor?" Lawrence asked.

Declan, with exaggerated gallantry, got to his feet and held out the fourth chair at our table for Yvette. Lawrence, meanwhile, filled another glass with wine.

"Eating the wrong sort of mushroom can produce a slow and painful death," Lawrence declared solemnly. "I don't know that I could bear to watch."

"Park probably knows more about mushrooms than the rest of us combined," I speculated.

"Let's just hope so," Declan said.

◆

A chronicle generally thought to be spurious and not likely to have been composed by Turpin, the archbishop of Reims, as it pretends to be, relates how the first pilgrim to make his way to the shrine of the Apostle was none other than the emperor Charlemagne. The king of the Franks was visited one night by the Apostle in a dream and exhorted to raise a great army with which to wrest back from the Moors that which they themselves had forcibly seized. Simply by following the stars of the Milky Way to Galicia, the emperor and his army would reach the tomb in which the earthly remains of the Apostle rested, thus establishing the route which others would then follow, in ever greater numbers, until the end of time.

"Go," urged the saint, according to the pseudo-Turpin, "and I will help you. And you will win from God celestial glory, and your name will remain in the memory of mankind for so long as the world itself endures."

It made a good story, even if the dates didn't add up. By the time of the rediscovery of the tomb of the Apostle in the Bosque de Libredón, Charlemagne was already at rest in his own tomb. As for Turpin, whom the chronicle credits with completing the work of the Apostle by baptizing the remaining pagans of Galicia, the archbishop too had perished well before related events, in a high mountain pass beyond Roncesvalles, alongside Roland.

Just beyond the walls of Pamplona was a field where a battle between Charlemagne's army and the Moors was said to have occurred, a battle in which so much blood was spilt that it took months for the earth to absorb it. The Camino would once have echoed with the tales of Charlemagne and Roland. On the very route of the *Vía Láctea* was a poplar forest said to have grown from the lances planted in the ground by the soldiers of Charlemagne when they paused there to rest.

◆

Yvette's story, which she began telling me the next morning as soon as we were once more on the road, was that she was the manageress of a shop in Paris, a jewellery shop situated in one of the more questionable parts of the city, where of late there had been many robberies. Once she had enjoyed her work, but now she found it both tedious and a great strain on account of having always to remain alert.

The road began to climb again, heading up towards the Alto del

Perdón.   Behind us, far in the distance, we could see other pilgrims spread out along the way. Over many years, by walking for two or three weeks at a time, Yvette had completed the pilgrim route from Paris to the Pyrenées, always returning to her work feeling refreshed and, for a time at least, somewhat more optimistic. Her plan was to continue walking in this fitful manner all the way across Spain, being in no particular hurry to reach Compostela, and even dreading the moment when she would actually arrive there.

Rain began to fall again and turned to snow as we neared the top of the hill. The wind was whistling and the rocky path had become treacherous. We had reached the site of the Fuente de Reniega, the Well of Renunciation, so called for an incident in which a pilgrim, although near to dying from thirst, had nevertheless refused to make a pact with the Devil in order to obtain water. The Apostle himself, as a consequence, had come to the aid of the steadfast pilgrim, and thus the legacy of the fountain.

On the hilltop was a line of metal pilgrims and animals, with an inscription that identified this as the place where the path of the wind crossed with that of the stars. Perhaps that was so, but those cut-out, cartoon-like figures would surely have been more at home in an amusement park or a children's playground.

We descended with care. Now and again I could feel Yvette, who was walking close behind, grab hold of my rucksack. If she were to fall on these rocks, she predicted, it was certain, with her luck, that she would break something.

"*Voilà votre optimisme*," I observed.

"*Voilà ma sagesse.*"

The weather having improved by the afternoon, we made a detour to visit the mysterious octagonal chapel and pilgrim burial ground at Eunate. Unfortunately, our arrival coincided with that of two large buses, one full of German tourists, the other transporting Spanish schoolchildren. No sooner were the students out of their bus than the boys lined up to urinate

into a hedge, a scene which a number of the Germans considered worthy
of a photograph.

"*Monstres!*" Yvette muttered.

"*Lesquels?*"

"*Tous les deux.*"

The chapel was surrounded by a cloister which we circled the
requisite number of times before entering, but there was no magic to
be found within on that day, nor any peace, nor any tranquillity, only
the stern German pastor and a very well-dressed Spanish schoolmistress
exchanging poisonous glances. So much for the hour of quiet meditation
recommended in our guidebooks.

Another hour of walking brought us to the town of Puente la Reina.
We stopped on the bridge from which the town took its name, a bridge
built there in the 11th century at the behest of the queen of that day.
Like Park, Yvette had her itinerary already worked out and it entailed her
continuing on rather than waiting there, as I intended to, for the others.
Having located a scrap of paper in one of the many pockets in her trousers,
she jotted down her address in Paris so that, if we failed to meet again, I
could send her a postcard when I arrived in Compostela. She kissed me
first on each cheek, and then lightly on the lips.

I remained where I was, giving her time to move off. Who you met
and came to befriend along the way was largely down to chance, which
required sufficient space in which to play itself out. On that bridge
meanwhile, where for more than a thousand years pilgrims had crossed
from one bank of the river to the other, I found it was surprisingly easy,
to lose oneself, to let go of one's own preoccupations, and so enter that
other stream, that human current which over time had left, on the bridge,
the imprint of its passing worn into the stones.

From their bunks Lawrence and Declan had watched Park get up that
morning, perform his packing ritual, and set out from the refuge, but
neither of them had seen him since. As Declan had made the detour to

Eunate and Lawrence hadn't, one or the other of them ought to have passed Park at some point along the way.

"On the other hand," Declan argued, " he can hardly expect one of us to be around to pull him out of every ditch that he falls into."

Lawrence's sole concern at the end of another long day "on the trail" was to find a bar in which to have a quiet drink. To find a bar, that is to say, in which the television wasn't turned up full blast.

"I've noticed that as well," said Declan. "Is everyone in this country deaf?"

"If they're not," said Lawrence, "they soon will be."

During the day the televisions were tuned either to soap operas or else, there in the north, to a game which, in Lawrence's description, consisted solely of two men in white trousers bouncing a ball off a wall.

"Our learned friend here", said Lawrence nodding in my direction, "can probably even tell you what it's called."

Pelota. It was a Basque game similar to handball, and we had passed a number of courts that day. There were walls on two sides of the court, with a stand for the spectators on the third side.

"Imagine that!" Declan exclaimed. "And here I was thinking that they must have run out of money before they finished it."

A further pilgrim route joined the Camino Francés in Puente la Reina, one which entered Spain to the east of Roncesvalles via the Somport pass. The *comedor* was crowded that evening as a result and the waiter was put out by our having moved two of the tables together without first asking his permission. Pilgrims did just as they pleased, he muttered to himself as he brought the bread, but some people still had to earn a living.

"*¡Hermanos!*"

The waiter ran towards Park wagging a finger. No rucksacks were allowed in the dining room, no walking sticks, no cagoules, and no dripping hats. Park, having left the offending items in the corridor, returned to tell us how, upon leaving the chapel of Eunate, which had impressed him greatly, he had set off in completely the wrong direction and ended up in a town that wasn't even on his map. Only by walking in the dark for an hour, by the light of a small torch, had he managed to complete the day's walk as he had planned.

In the notes which I made before going to sleep that night, I was drawn back to the notion of the Camino with its endless flow of pilgrims being like a river. Those whom the Camino favoured were more or less carried along by the current right from the beginning, whereas the lot of others, even those who might have been the better swimmers, was constantly to struggle.

FIND YOUR OWN WAY

✠

*There is no one so prone to believing too little
as those who began by believing too much.*

Miguel de Unamuno

Any pilgrim wishing to make a pilgrimage to Compostela would have
been obliged, before setting off, to put his affairs in order. No debts
or any animosities were to be left behind. He would have been well advised
also to forgive any debts still owed to him by others. The departing pilgrim
was also required to make a will and secure the permission of his wife and
local priest, agreeing with the former in the presence of the latter on how
long, should he fail to return, she needed to wait before remarrying.

To help him on his way and to ward off dogs and wolves, he would
need to carry a sturdy staff, a *bordón*, which was for the pilgrim his
third leg. A broad-brimmed hat offered protection against the rain and
sun, and whatever was his outermost garment during the day would in
addition serve as his blanket by night. His belongings he packed into
a satchel made from hide which he had been warned not to bind with
ties but to leave open, thus demonstrating his willingness to share with
others.

Meals might be few and far apart. Hung from his staff, to tide him
over, would be a gourd filled with wine and tucked away in his satchel
a chunk of bread so hard that it could neither be sliced with a knife nor
bitten into, but had to be grated with a grater. And thus the *copla*:

Con pan y con vino, se anda camino.

Apart from wives travelling with their husbands, pilgrims were mainly
men. Of female pilgrims in general, Pope Boniface remarked that a great

many perished and that few kept their virtue, and a Spanish proverb concurred: *Ir romera, volver ramera*. Go a pilgrim, return a whore.

Of those who set off for Compostela, not all did so of their own volition. *Peregrinos forzados* were those sentenced to a pilgrimage as punishment for an offence committed. A male offender could be sentenced to walk naked; a female offender would walk clad in white. A murderer could be shackled with manacles forged from the metal of his murder weapon.

Some walked the Camino on behalf of others. Where old age, illness, or death prevented a pilgrimage from being completed, a son might substitute for a father, or a nephew for an uncle, or else a stranger might need to be employed. And thus *peregrinos a sueldo*, salaried pilgrims.

◆

The Camino, in finding its way across the north of Spain, would have sought the line of least resistance, the route later favoured by highways. The way west from Puente la Reina was subject to various detours as the pilgrim road was diverted around the massive excavations being undertaken in preparation for the laying down of another sort of route. Added to the irritation of the mud and the extra kilometres was the constant looming presence of heavy earth-moving equipment, the size and power of which dwarfed and appeared to mock the puniness of the solitary walker.

There was little enthusiasm for the new project in the small bar where I stopped for lunch. Business was good at the moment, with so many workmen about, but once the new highway was completed, as there was no exit planned for miles in either direction, the bar would have to close.

"What can we do," the proprietor asked, "if everyone is in so much of a hurry? You can't argue with God or the government."

An elderly man standing at the bar turned to face me.

"And you, for example. Where are you from? Are you German?"

"I'm from many places," I replied, "but I live in Scotland."

"Ah, Scotland." The old man rubbed the stubble on his cheeks. "And what country does Scotland neighbour with?"

Scotland, someone else thought, bordered with Norway. The proprietor, as he put down my sandwich, made a gesture of helplessness. If this was how little they knew of the world now, he reflected, what would happen there once the highway had been completed, and the bar had disappeared, and not even pilgrims any longer paused there?

I had met the woman briefly the evening before in the refuge, where she had been trying to get the Internet machine to work. She was young, in her thirties, and had walked alone all the way from Switzerland, entering Spain through the Somport Pass. We met up for the second time that afternoon at a village fountain, where we had both stopped for a rest.

Her name was Angelika. She wore her long blonde hair in a braid and spoke English with a German accent, but she was no friend of the German pilgrims that she had met so far, as they teased her, calling her "Heidi."

We compared our maps, agreeing that there were another nine kilometres still to go to get to Estella and the next refuge, at which point a woman in an apron sweeping the street in front of her house approached us. No, it wasn't nine kilometres to Estella, but only *ocho*, eight. She knew because her sister lived there.

I thanked her and congratulated her on having been able to understand our English. Not the words, she admitted, only the numbers. She had learned in school how to count to ten in English and she still practiced counting from time to time *por si acaso*, just in case.

As we walked on Angelika told me about how a waiter in a restaurant, noticing that she was struggling to understand the *menú del día*, had taken her into the kitchen and pointed out to her the various dishes on the menu as they were still being prepared. She was impressed by the friendliness of the Spanish, and by their helpfulness, but not by their efficiency.

"Imagine letting a guest go into the kitchen! Why not prepare the menu in more than one language?"

I suggested that perhaps the waiter had merely been fond of blondes.

"That should not be allowed, not while he is on duty."

She herself, until recently, had worked in a hotel and had been in charge of fifty other people, so she knew that it was sometimes necessary to be strict. Being strict with others, however, meant being even more strict with yourself.

"And then one day you wake up," Angelika said, shading her eyes from the sinking sun, "and you can no longer remember who you used to be."

The town of Estella, Estella la Bella, was one of those places which had come into being specifically for the convenience of those walking the Camino. According to the earliest of the pilgrim guides, Estella overflowed with all delights. By that evening, as on every evening, the Camino had deposited there the latest cohort of an ever-changing company of pilgrims.

I accompanied Park on a visit to one of the town's churches, and afterwards we sat talking in the cloister. Since becoming a Catholic, Park claimed, he had never questioned anything that the Church taught, not the dogma, not the miracles of the saints, not the infallibility of the Pope, nothing. Some of the teachings of the Church he considered to be obviously true and the rest he had simply taken on faith.

"You have a great deal more trust than I do, " I remarked, "in the powers that be."

"God would never deceive us, brother."

"That's not the power I had in mind."

Sparrows were nesting in the cloister. Now and again a sparrow flew down with a bit of grass or straw in its beak. The nest was under an eave, protected from the weather and also from cats. If birds could look after themselves in this way, I argued, without any need to imagine a deity, then why couldn't we?

Park reflected for a moment, regarding the sparrows, and then he asked if I had any children. Not to my knowledge, I replied. The manner of my own upbringing had robbed me of any desire to bring up children of my own.

"I have two," Park said, "and how could I discipline them if I didn't believe that God laid down rules for us to live by? Without God's law everything would be arbitrary, and we would all go our own way."

"And don't we, in the end?"

No one, Park insisted, could look after even himself, much less after others, all of the time. Whether as a father or a surgeon, if he were left to take all the responsibility for everything onto himself alone, he would find life impossible.

"God loves us, *hermano*. It's because I know this that my hand doesn't shake when I spank my children or cut out a cancer."

◆

When and how, according to the mythology of Santiago, did the scallop shell come to be the emblem of the pilgrim to Compostela? It was in the days of Bishop Teodomiro, the first to have proclaimed the tomb found in the forest of Libredón to be that of the Apostle. One story relates how a man was riding home on horseback along a stretch of beach near to where, many centuries before, the vessel bearing the sacred remains of the Apostle had first reached the shore of Galicia, when suddenly, from out of the sea, a monstrous creature reared up and swept the helpless rider from his mount and into the green waves. Or might it not have been the sea itself which seized the horseman, as from time to time the sea today still carries off an unfortunate fisherman or an unwary tourist from that shore?

The victim was no swimmer, and, what was worse, was just returning from an amorous encounter and so was in a state of mortal sin, his flesh still having dominion over his spirit. Nevertheless, finding himself at the very threshold of the other world, the drowning man called out to Santiago for mercy, and not in vain. In an instant the sea was parted in two, exposing a sandy bottom covered with seaweed, scallop shells, and snails. The Holy Apostle approached, bathed in a beautiful light, and lifted the senseless body tenderly off the seabed. The saint then entrusted it to the gentlest of swells, to be carried safely back to the shore.

Returned to his senses, and having been delivered from the fury of the sea, the horseman found clinging to his clothing that most beautiful of shells, the *venera*, which in the former mythology of the Greeks as well as that of the Romans had been the cradle of a goddess, of Aphrodite and then Venus. Deposed as a symbol of female fecundity, the scallop shell would subsequently become the emblem of a pilgrim to the sepulchre of the Apostle James, and what better to signify the pilgrim's own trials, and his own encounter with the saint, than a sign said to have been given to a drowning man snatched from the waves?

◆

Park, who had refrained from unpacking his rucksack completely the night before, was ready and waiting to set out with me the next morning at dawn. In the faint light Park appeared larger than life, and with his wide hat and heavy wooden *bordón* might easily have been mistaken for a character in an oriental print.

The way out of Estella took us past more construction work. An immense crane was already at work lowering a prefabricated wall onto the uppermost floor of a half-finished apartment block. Luxury living, a sign promised. One, two, and three bedroom apartments, all with balconies overlooking the Camino de Santiago and with underground parking included.

"Heaven," I remarked sourly, "on earth."

"Didn't you sleep well last night, brother?" Park asked cheerfully.

A path branched off in the direction of the monastery of Irache, which had once housed a monk called Veremundo, a monk renowned for feeding pilgrims and the poor, who, when there was nothing else to give, even gave away food intended for his brother monks. Across the valley meanwhile a line of cliffs was just catching the first rays of the sun, and had begun to glow with an eerie white light.

Adjacent to the monastery, and carrying on the tradition of hospitality to pilgrims, was a *bodega*, a winery at the gates of which a "wine fountain" was maintained, a tap from which pilgrims were invited to help themselves. Park dug out his camera, but then thought better of it: his wife back in Korea, whom he phoned every other night, was already convinced that he was drinking more wine than was good for him.

We filled our cups and sat down to rest. Park's son was in his first year of university, and his daughter was entering university the following year.

"My wife worries that something might happen to me, and there won't be enough money. In Korea, it's the wife who controls the finances."

Before setting off on this trip he had never even had a bank card, and he still wasn't quite certain how to use one. What if the card wasn't recognized, and the machine refused to return it to him? He still had plenty of money, which he kept in a body wallet strapped to his chest, but sooner or later he would need to access the special account which his wife had set up for him.

"She's afraid that I'll lose the card, brother, or that someone will steal it, so she only puts into the account as much as we could do without."

Park wanted to have a look at the monastery while we were there, but the doors were still locked. It was too early for the monastery, but not for wine. The sun, a warm Spanish sun, had in any case risen above the trees by this time and was beckoning us on.

As we walked, Park returned to the subject which we had been discussing the evening before. At that very moment, whether we wanted it that way or not, there was someone, Park insisted, looking over our shoulders.

"Haven't you ever sensed that, brother?"

I said that I had never been given the opportunity to sense God for myself, having from an early age had a fully worked out concept of God imposed upon me. God was good, and it was God who had made the world, the reasoning went, and therefore the world was good, and all else, unhappiness, misfortune, illness, evil, and even death, was a matter of human error. Nothing that afflicted humankind was real, but only a disorder of thought. Such had been the religious belief of my mother, before which my father, uncharacteristically, had remained tactfully silent.

"Children are weak, brother. Children need to be protected."

"And if children are protected with wishful thinking, how will they defend themselves as adults?"

Once the premise had been accepted, the reasoning was relentless. One became ill by accepting the reality of illness. Among the causes of illness were doctors, hospitals, medical plans, and whatever else served to make us fearful. Aspirin caused headaches, x-rays caused cancer. Such, given the reticence of my father, had been my own first take on the world.

"You mustn't blame God," Park reproached me, "for what isn't God's doing."

It was as though we had leap-frogged spring right into summer. The sun was hot by now, the sky was a faultless blue, and Park, who had not yet lost any weight, was by midday ready for a nap. He had enjoyed our talk, he said as he removed his boots and socks, and he hoped that I would bear in mind what we had discussed.

"Don't worry," I said, tapping the small notebook which I carried in the pocket of my shirt. "It all ends up here."

We divided up the bread and cheese which we had bought for lunch. I wanted to keep going, maintaining the rhythm which was becoming second nature to me. My reason for writing down each day's events in the evening, I explained to Park, was in order to have a complete record of the Camino: the good, the bad, the strange, the surprising, the disconcerting.

"Not forgetting," I added, "fatigue, discomfort, and tedium."

"And all in such a small notebook, brother?"

"When it's full I'll mail it home and buy another."

The Italian woman who ran the *albergue* in Torres del Río was sitting out in the street when I arrived, chatting with a neighbour about a television program which they had all seen the night before.

"What can we do?" the neighbour remarked. "We can only watch what they show. They must think that we are stupid."

"But here at least," the *hospitalera* pointed out, "we can also watch pilgrims."

The first of the others to appear that afternoon was the Swiss pilgrim, Angelika. I had by this time showered and washed my clothes and was sitting out in the sun, beside the rack on which my clothes were drying.

"How is it inside?" Angelika demanded, peering in a window of the refuge. "Is it clean? Is there hot water? I have been perspiring very much indeed today."

"There's everything you could wish for, including a mop and bucket in the shower."

"And is there just one shower for everyone?"

"For men, for women, you name it."

"In that case I will mop also *before* my shower."

This, we all agreed, had been the best day yet. To each their own Camino, but a day in the countryside, under a full sun, was a universal joy. That evening, with Park in the lead and with several of the others tagging along, we went in search of the key for the village's one tourist attraction, another of those mysterious octagonal chapels. The woman who had charge of the key, even though quite elderly, insisted on accompanying us, and while the others were looking around she motioned me to one side.

"*Aquel chino,*" she wanted to know, indicating Park, "*¿es cristiano?*"

"*Más que nadie,*" I assured her. Very much so.

"*¿Católico?*" the woman persisted, "*o ¿protestante?*"

Attempts had been made to link that chapel with the Templars. Someone pointed out what certainly appeared to be an Arab arch. Angelika, when we were ready to leave, asked me if we ought to give something to the woman with the key, or if it was sufficient just to buy a few postcards.

◆

The Church of Saint James was consecrated in Compostela in 899, and incorporated marble brought north from Moorish Spain during the winter truces. Compostela probably meant "little cemetery." A religious community had sprung up, adjacent to the church, to welcome the pilgrims who had begun to flock there, and in just over a hundred years that first church had become a cathedral.

Nothing needed to be invented, the model already existed elsewhere, in France, in the monastery of Cluny, where it was the cult of Saint Martin which attracted pilgrims and raised revenues. Wherever in Christendom a relic of a saint had been preserved, a miracle book was kept in which the wondrous workings of the sacred remnants were recorded, which served to attract not only more pilgrims to the site, but also, no doubt, to structure the experiences with the saint which they themselves would subsequently relate to others.

By the twelfth century a work had been compiled which was at once a miracle book, a guide book, and a first history of the pilgrimage to Compostela. Thus, through the *Liber Sancti Jacob*, also known as the *Codex Calixtinus*, the Camino was both popularised and facilitated. And thus, in the style of the day, the following picture drawn with words:

> Thither to the Apostle's tomb betake themselves the rich,
> robbers, horsemen, pedestrians, princes, the blind, the lame,
> the prosperous, noblemen, squires, people of rank,
> bishops, abbots, some barefooted, some without means,
> others burdened with iron for reasons of repentance.

"*Cargados con hierros*," the Spanish rendering has it, "*con motivos de penetencia*." To each their own Camino, then as now.

◆

I preferred, at times, having the Camino to myself. The bar in Torres del Río opened early in the morning especially for pilgrims, but I didn't dally, preferring to set off while the others were still sipping their coffee.

I climbed the hill behind the village and then paused to watch the sun as it rose behind me, lighting the valley and the hills beyond.

Walking beside a forest later, I heard a woodpecker, and I tried to recall what that bird was called in Spanish. I was no longer concerned about becoming lost, or suffering an injury while walking alone. The evening before, Angelika had told me about an encounter with a snake on the path which had left her paralysed with fear. She had to wait for another pilgrim to come along and move it out the way for her with his stick.

"He said to me that the snake was not even poisonous, but I am thinking still that he might have been wrong."

Suddenly it came to me: *pájaro carpintero*. Carpenter bird. For years I had studied Spanish, and I had lived for short periods both in Mexico and Spain, but for some reason I had never learned the language properly. Rightly or wrongly I associated this failing with my earlier failure, despite years of lessons, to learn to play the cello.

Coming into the town of Viana, with its cobbled streets, I found myself, to my surprise, being hailed in English.

"Good day! I see that you're still at it."

She was seated by herself on the terrace of a bar, at a table strewn with sheets of paper. Summoning the waiter, she ordered two beers, in excellent Spanish, and a *tapa* of olives. The sheets, I saw as she shuffled them together, contained the sketches which she had made since setting out from Roncesvalles on the bus.

"Sheila, wasn't it?" I ventured. "The Aussie?"

"Got it in one. Didn't I tell you we'd meet up again?"

She motioned me to a chair. She was in her fifties, and bright crimson was probably no longer the true colour of her close-cropped hair. She had walked the Camino for the first time several years earlier, she told me by way of explaining the sketches, and had found it not just an overwhelming experience, but also one completely beyond her comprehension.

"To me, understanding something means being able to draw it. So here I am back again, and this time with a sketch pad."

She passed me the drawing which she had just completed. It showed a pilgrim walking towards a hilltop village; above the roofs of the village could be seen the bell tower of a church. At the bottom of the sketch was a caption, in Spanish, to the effect that to walk the Camino was to pray with one's feet.

The *comedor* of the bar was small, with no more than half a dozen tables, and the choices on the day's *menú* were few, but these were authentic Spanish dishes, Sheila pointed out, and not the bland fare usually served up to pilgrims.

Almost from the start, when first walking the Camino, she had been aware of an unusual energy rising up from the earth, an energy which she had been able to feel right through her boots. The further she walked, the stronger she seemed to become, and she had at the same time been possessed of a greatly heightened sense of awareness.

"We call it crystal clarity…"

"Crystal clarity?"

"The ability to see through bullshit."

We were by now started on our bread and wine. The very act of walking, I argued, any effort at all in fact, could be therapeutic. A physical rhythm was established which in turn imposed a salutary and calming rhythm on the mind. This was no doubt the case, Sheila conceded, but it was no explanation. Knowledge gathered concerning fireflies, no matter how accurate, would never explain lightning.

A platter of green peas and *serrano* ham was placed between us to be shared. The Australian aborigines had long known what the rest of us were only just discovering, Sheila continued as we went to work on the *primer plato*. Certain sites and features of the earth gave off special forms of energy, and human beings could not only sense this energy but also learn how to benefit from it.

"That knowledge appears in their stories," she added, "as well as in their art. It's there for anyone, there for the taking."

We made short work of the peas and ham. Using her napkin, Sheila brushed the crumbs of bread on the table into a small pile, making room for the next dish, *churrasco*, grilled meat, in this case pork ribs. Unfortunately not many aborigines were any longer able to channel the energy of the earth, as there were very few places where the features of the earth had been left undisturbed.

"And that goes for Spain as well," Sheila added. "Have you noticed all the cranes?"

"And jumbo earth-movers. Everything's being picked up and taken somewhere else."

"And nothing suffocates the healing energy of the earth quicker than asphalt."

The afternoon was fine. Sheila, who had intended to go on by taxi, now decided to walk the next stretch of the Camino instead, rather than interrupt our chat.

"Providing, of course, that you don't think I'm completely bonkers."

"No," I said, being glad again to have company. "Not completely."

Her rucksack was already packed. Her sketches and her sketch pad she carried separately, in a quilted carry-all. On her head she wore an Aussie bush hat. Her biggest mistake in life, she said, was to have married too young, and, even worse, to have married her very first boyfriend.

"Before I knew it I had three children plus a good-for-nothing husband to look after. To this day I don't know how I managed to stay sane."

The first six years had been just about bearable because at least the sex was good, but the remaining eighteen years had been a nightmare. Not until the last of the children had been safely shipped off to university, however, had her husband finally agreed to a divorce.

"It was to mark the end of that life that I decided to do the Camino."

From the very first day she had felt like a different person. Finding herself in new situations, and in the company of interesting people, she had felt recharged and energized. It wasn't until she returned home to

Melbourne, however, and met up with a woman whom she had known for many years, that she suddenly recognized that this was the person with whom she wanted to share the rest of her life.

"And how did your kids take that?" I inquired.

"They were completely wiped out. My daughter asked, in tears, if it was hereditary."

The energy of the Camino, she had since come to realize, was neutral. It wasn't a matter of being directed one way or another, but rather of being stimulated to consider possibilities which you might for one reason or another never have dared to consider previously.

"Without the Camino I might never have noticed what now seems so obvious. It's much less difficult loving someone who's more like yourself."

We crossed the Ebro, Spain's greatest river, and entered the city of Logroño, which was just coming back to life again after the midday siesta. Fortunately there were still plenty of beds left at the refuge, and Sheila, despite not having any pilgrim credentials, managed to talk herself into one.

"Two things I learned the last time," she confided. "You're likely to get a little more of what you ask for here if you ask for it in Spanish, and rules, here, are made to be bent."

◆

From Cluny, along with much else, came the Benedictine tradition of hospitality. Every pilgrim and visitor, Benedict's Rule required, was to be received as Christ himself would have been received. Pilgrim hospitals started to appear along the road to Compostela, offering accommodation for the healthy as well as the infirm, which led to the tradition, today, of pilgrims being looked after by *hospitaleros*.

Hospitality was expected from all, as many pilgrim stories bear witness. So we hear of how a starving pilgrim begging for bread at the door of a hut was once refused by a woman with the excuse that she had no bread, even though a loaf of bread was at that very moment baking in the ashes of her fire.

The pilgrim, disappointed, went on his way, but as he did so the bread which the woman had denied having was miraculously transformed; when she went to retrieve the loaf from the ashes, she found that it had been turned to stone. In vain she ran after the pilgrim to beg for his forgiveness, but he was nowhere to be seen. So, in this fashion did a lie, through the intercession of the Apostle, become the truth.

By the eleventh century, thanks to road works undertaken by King Alonso VI of Castilla y León and King Sancho Ramírez of Navarro y Aragon, the pilgrim route had become fixed. New villages and towns began to spring up, settlements whose single long street, whose Calle Mayor, was nothing more nor less than the Camino itself.

Bridges were built to span the rivers, and stretches of ancient road were reclaimed where necessary from the forest or a morass. Where there were conflicts, pilgrims were guaranteed safe passage, and where they could be distinguished from merchants, pilgrims travelling to the tomb of the Apostle were granted freedom from tolls.

By the 12th century half a million pilgrims a year were finding their way to Galicia. In bringing a river of the faithful to that impoverished corner of Christendom, the Camino provided an infusion of prosperity for a stagnant economy, serving as a lifeline for the birth of a new Spain, a redeemed Spain, a Christian Spain. Inns and wineshops sprang up along the route, and a special dispensation was granted to bootmakers, allowing them to repair the boots of pilgrims on Sundays.

◆

Another of Sheila's sketches had shown a pilgrim only from behind, kneeling to drink from a spring, the caption at the bottom of the sheet reading : "*El Camino a cada cual le da lo que necesita.*" The Camino gives to each what is required. The mottos which she used as her captions were borrowed, or were rather the common property of all pilgrims, as they could be found in any refuge, scribbled into its *Libro de Peregrino* by someone who had stayed the night there. Modern day pilgrims, like those who had preceded them, clearly found comfort in the thought that something other than their own efforts alone was at play on the Camino, and all would therefore be well.

We were now in Rioja country, the region and thus the name of its wine coming from the name of a river, the Río Oja. On the track westwards from Logroño, a cuckoo seemed to be accompanying me, calling to me repeatedly, although remaining out of sight in the scrub. The gentle rise and fall of the land, as well as the company of the bird, did indeed suggest to me on that morning, that all must be well with the world.

Several hours after my first breakfast on nuts and dates, I reached a bar whose proprietress was happy to prepare me a tortilla. As she whipped the eggs, she asked why I was walking alone and if I ever felt lonely.

"*Más vale solo,*" says a handy Spanish proverb, "*que mal acompañado.*"

Better alone than poorly accompanied. A pilgrim was never alone for long, I explained, and would soon make friends with whom to pass the evenings. It was no different from going out to work each morning and then returning home at the end of the day to the bosom of one's family.

She herself, the woman remarked as she folded over the omelette, would have felt lonely and probably frightened walking alone, and she then asked me, as did old men in bars and farmers whom I passed in their fields, if I were German.

"*Soy escocés. Es decir, vivo en Edimburgo.*"

"*Ah, Edimburgo. Y Edimburgo*", the woman persisted, "*¿no está en Alemania?*"

I had now been a week on the road and I had walked, on average, better than twenty-five kilometres a day. Each evening I noted down anything of interest that I had seen that day, chapels, statues, ruins, rivers, the grave of Cesar Borgia, but what I took most care over, and what was filling up the majority of the pages of my notebook, were conversations.

The historic capital of the Rioja region was the town of Nájara. Sprawled on the grass in front of the refuge, waiting for it to open, were a number of American pilgrims whom I hadn't seen before but who were soon confiding that they had walked only a few miles that day. They were all from the same church in Michigan and they were doing the Camino, or as much of it as they had time for, in order to spread world peace.

"And how are you doing *that?*" I inquired.

"By talking to other pilgrims. We expected it to be hard, but you'd be surprised how many of them speak English."

Angelika, who had been passed on the road by their bus, was furious when she realized that the Americans were being allowed to stay at the refuge. They had waved to her, she fumed, out the windows.

"How can they call themselves pilgrims if they never walk? Do you know that some of them have their guitars with them?"

"Perhaps they'll be singing folksongs later. They're here to promote world peace."

"World peace, that is very funny indeed. I think they must be here because where they come from no one will listen."

We went for a beer before the evening meal. Angelika also carried a notebook and wrote in it at the end of each day in the most minuscule German. The two of us sitting together, bent over our notebooks, discouraged others from intruding.

She had been too angry at the Americans and their bus to notice the sign that greeted pilgrims where the Camino entered the town. I passed her my notes for the day so that she could copy it. The sign had read:

Peregrinos, en Nájera, najerinos.

Not just the sentiment was to be admired, but the concision:
Pilgrims, when in Nájera, you're one of us.

SHIP OF FOOLS

✝

Life is, in itself and forever, shipwreck.

José Ortega y Gasset

Along the Way of Saint James there was scarcely a bridge or a town without a tale to tell. At every turn the pilgrim company encountered sites pregnant with meaning, a constant reminder that theirs was an undertaking of more than mere earthly significance. Even as their feet were carrying them towards their goal, the faithful were being prepared for what they would find, and for what they would receive, when they knelt before the tomb of the Apostle.

The route between Logroño and Burgos had been made easier for the pilgrim through the efforts of Santo Domingo de la Calzada, a builder of roads and bridges as well as, even in his own lifetime, a worker of miracles. Using only a small sickle he had cleared an entire forest, afterwards planting vineyards where only a wilderness had been, and founding the city which would bear his name and which was later to become the site of the best known of all the miracle stories to which the pilgrimage gave rise.

A family of German pilgrims arrived in the city one day, a husband and wife, with their son, a handsome lad who soon caught the eye of one of the servants in the inn where the family was to spend the night. As soon as it was dark the girl sought out the youth where he was sleeping and attempted to slip into the bed beside him, only to be pushed away.

"I've come to seek salvation," the pious youth made it clear, "not to be stained by foul intercourse!"

Furious at having been scorned, the servant set out to take revenge. Having first secreted a silver cup amongst the belongings of the unfortunate youth, she then reported it missing. A search was made, the cup was found and the youth was brought before the mayor of the city to be sentenced for the crime of theft, the penalty for which, anywhere on the Camino, was hanging.

The youth's protestations fell on deaf ears, and the tears of his distraught parents might just as well have been rain. Only when they arrived in the city of Santiago and related all that had occurred to a priest, were the bereaved parents offered consolation.

"A grave injustice has been done," the priest concurred. "But you must leave everything in the hands of the one whom you have come here to honour."

On returning from the city of the Apostle, the couple found themselves once more entering the city of Santo Domingo de la Calzada. There they came upon their son still hanging from the scaffold, and to their amazement he was still alive. A grave miscarriage of justice had miraculously been averted, and the couple went at once to inform the mayor, who was just sitting down to his midday meal.

"Your son?" he said. "Still alive? Are you insane? Your son is no more alive than this fat hen that I'm about to enjoy."

At which point the fowl, although cooked through, stirred itself on the platter and began to cackle. By this means justice was done in the end, and thus the famous lines which serve the city still as its motto:

Santo Domingo de la Calzada,
donde cantó la gallina después de asada.

Santo Domingo de la Calzada, where the roasted chicken still clucked.

◆

Beyond Nájera the road began to climb. The rain was falling steadily, and the wind was blowing directly into the face of any pilgrim walking west. Not today was there any delight in a sunrise, or any cuckoo serenade.

The story of the young man saved from the gallows in Santo Domingo de la Calzada, the very place which I was now approaching, had a sequel.

The mayor, as punishment for his not having investigated the case properly in the first place, was required to wear a cord knotted in the manner of a noose around his own neck, and to share his every midday meal after that with a pilgrim. Also, in the cathedral of the city, a pair of caged chickens were to this day kept on display, a living reminder, if by no means a proof, of the miracle said once to have occurred there.

I had just reached the cathedral, the front doors of which were locked, when Declan caught up with me. We agreed that we could hardly pass by without a look inside, even if this meant chasing after the key.

"But I was just thinking," said Declan, "that we might let some of this water drip off us first while we're sipping a *tinto*."

We sipped several *tintos*. The bar was as warm as you like, and with every additional glass of wine that we ordered, a different sort of *tapa* was set before us.

"Isn't it a bloody miracle how much people eat in this country," Declan remarked, "before they even sit down to a meal?"

Declan, in just a week's time, would be back in Dublin, getting married to his childhood sweetheart. He was twenty-eight years old and he had decided that it was now or never, both for the wedding and for fitting in as much as he could of the Camino.

"A married man can't just go off like this, not to begin with anyway. He needs to show himself first to be a worthwhile member of society, or so I've been informed."

Now that we were out of the rain, he was once more wearing a cap that his mother had knitted especially for his travels. His mother, never having visited Spain, had been somewhat in the dark, according to Declan. Thus the resemblance of his pilgrim cap to a tea cosy.

We made our way back to the cathedral. The great front doors were still closed, but a young woman with an armful of flowers was going in through a side door and I asked her if we could get in that way as well to see the chickens. Declan, whose Spanish extended no further than improvisations, added a few clucking sounds.

"Of course," the woman said, "but you're no longer allowed to feed them."

The tradition had once been for pilgrims to feed a few crumbs of bread to the birds and then to pluck out a white feather each to wear in their hats, but the number of pilgrims was now too great. Feathers could now be purchased in the cathedral shop.

The cage contained a cock and a hen, and the birds were changed every six weeks. Some priests in the past had wanted to get rid of the birds as they disrupted the mass, in particular the early morning mass, but the priests, the woman proudly recounted, had been over-ruled.

Before leaving, we each shook her hand. Coincidently, she was there to decorate the church for a wedding, and I asked her if she was, by chance, the one about to be married.

"No, it's not me. I'm married already. Today my sister goes into the cage."

The refuge at Grañon, the first of the "authentic" refuges of which I had been told, was in the bell tower of the village church. There were no beds in sight, only some exercise mats stacked in the corner of the room. A female pilgrim was already stretched out on the floor, peering at me from her sleeping bag with such a pained look on her face that I felt obliged to ask if she was all right.

"Not really," she replied. "Today I was given an injection which was supposed to make me feel better, but the pain has not stopped."

She was suffering from tendonitis in one knee and she had been taken that day by the village priest to a doctor in the neighbouring town. She was Dutch, her name was Rita, and she had been advised not to resume walking for at least three days.

"And then, if the swelling has not gone down, I must return home. What do you think of that?"

More boots could be heard on the staircase, and the room began to fill. Rita, the invalid, rolled over and turned her face to the wall.

"What's the matter with her?" Lawrence wanted to know. "She hasn't been drinking the water, has she?"

The *hospitalero*, an elderly Spaniard who was charged with preparing a communal meal, appeared at a loss as to how to proceed. He had been told to expect half a dozen pilgrims, but at least thirty were by this time crowded into the tower. Angelika, having found him in the kitchen making a desultory inventory of just what foodstuffs were on hand, decided that she herself would need to organize the meal.

"Who will shop?" she demanded. "I have here already a list."

I roped in Declan, who was more than willing, and Lawrence, who agreed only under duress. The *hospitalero*, obviously relieved, handed over a wad of notes, asking only that we get receipts.

The church bell was tolling by the time we returned, summoning the villager to evening mass. A small door in the tower opened directly into the choir loft, where we found the Dutch woman wrapped in a blanket.

"That friend of yours is very bossy," she complained. "She told me that I had to help in the kitchen if I wanted to eat."

"You don't suppose that she could be referring to Angelika, do you?" Declan said.

"Angelic little Angelika?" echoed Lawrence.

"Maybe you are all hypocrites," Rita snapped back. "But I'm Dutch, and we Dutch people say just what we think."

Paolo turned up again that evening, still wearing Lawrence's scarf. He told us that for the past few nights, in order to save money, he had been sleeping rough, and eating nothing but potatoes, having received a sack of them from an old woman in return for splitting firewood for her stove.

Three bowls were carried in from the kitchen, one overflowing with salad, another heaped with spaghetti noodles, and a third containing a pasta sauce made from tomatoes, onions, garlic, *pancetas*, and *chorizo*. Already on the table were two large baskets of bread and, to start with, half a dozen bottles of wine.

We toasted the cook. We toasted the *hospitalero*. We toasted Spain. Recalling Santo Domingo de la Calzada, we then toasted the road-building saint, the miracle of the roasted chicken, Declan's mother, Declan's cap, and his soon-to-be bride.

We were all agreed that this was indeed an authentic refuge. Those of us seated around that long table would later be sleeping shoulder to shoulder on the floor of the room below. In Paolo's opinion, generally speaking, Spain had nevertheless been a much better country when more of the population had been poor. Spain's new-found prosperity, like Portugal's, had spoiled the country, as all that people wanted to do now that they had a little money in their pockets, was to show off.

"Today I passed a field where a woman was ploughing with a team of oxen," Paolo gave as an example. "The foreign pilgrims stopped to take photographs, but the Spanish ones looked away, ashamed."

Meanwhile something was wrong in the kitchen. Angelika, who had gone for the remainder of her pasta sauce, was making signs from the doorway for me to join her. She was flushed and furious.

"Just look what they've done!" She indicated the empty saucepan. "How could anyone be so selfish!"

A Spanish family was also staying the night there, and had been provided with a room of their own. Instead of joining us or going out to a restaurant for their evening meal, it appeared that they had simply helped themselves to what had been left simmering on the stove, and Angelika, who was trembling with rage, wanted me to go with her to their room to confront them with what they had done.

I thought it a better idea just to hold her until she calmed down.

"They're just tourists," I told her. "They don't know any different. As for you, you've had a real triumph tonight, so why spoil it?"

Her body, after weeks of walking, was nothing but muscle, and every muscle in her body was taut. It felt as if I had hold of a coiled spring.

"Okay," she said after a time. "I agree with you. This is not like real life, this is only a game. There is no need to bite off the head of anyone."

She slumped, like a rag doll, when I released her into a chair. She was about the age that any daughter of my own would have been by now, if I had one.

"No need whatsoever," I agreed.

◆

Where there was no hospital in which to stay the night, the pilgrim had no choice but to find an inn, and warnings abound in the *Codex* as to the tricks and deceits of innkeepers. For the poor pilgrim a "bed" at an inn was a floor covered with straw which he shared with others. Innkeepers were forbidden to admit to their establishments any more pilgrims than they could accommodate, but who was to say, when the bed was the floor, just when that bed had been filled?

An inn at which white wine was available displayed a bundle of straw above the door, one dispensing *tinto* put out a red flag. Pilgrims who were greeted effusively on the threshold of an inn with a sample of the innkeeper's best wine, might nevertheless be served, once they had entered, with cider or vinegar.

In the marketplace pilgrims bought the necessary ingredients for the meals which they themselves would cook. An inn provided only cooking pots, utensils, salt, and a fire. A bath would have been out of the question (that's what rivers were for) and the clothing of many a pilgrim, by the time that he reached Compostela, would have been rotting away. For the poorer pilgrim, fleas and lice would have been his intimate companions.

Pilgrims kept up their spirits with songs. Singing lightened their load and shortened the road. In pilgrim songs, as in work songs, can still be found the cadences, virtually the very heartbeats, of those who first sang them.

An exhausted pilgrim, arriving at a monastery, might be given the loan of a *burro* for the succeeding stage of the journey. A pilgrim who was sick, sensing that the end of his journey was near, might dictate a *testamento* for which a priest or a *hospitalero* would serve as executor.

There were said to be certain trees along the route, the shade of which instantly restored a pilgrim's strength. Water taken from certain wells and hidden springs would, in a similarly miraculous way, restore his belief and sense of purpose.

Nor was even a lone pilgrim ever completely alone. Many a pilgrim, exhausted and near to despair, was brought back to his feet and to his senses, at a time when the great majority of pilgrims were still men, by the sudden appearance of a beautiful and mysterious woman on the path before him, beckoning him onwards.

◆

I was awakened, as always, by the sound of whispered conversations in German, and by the rustle of plastic bags. Small beams of light played on the walls. Angelika, whose mat was just beside mine, mumbled a complaint and burrowed deeper into her sleeping bag. Every morning, in every refuge, as if by a law of nature, there was a party of German pilgrims who rose before anyone else and set off in the dark.

Before setting off myself, I had breakfast in the kitchen with Paolo. We fried some bread left over from the night before, and shared a teabag. Outside in the corridor was a *donativo* box with no latch on it, just a sign: "*Deja lo que puedes y toma lo que necesitas.*" Give what you can, take what you need. Paolo was dismissive of this, saying that, in his opinion, it was an invitation to steal.

"Why don't they put on a lock? Suppose someone does go off with something? Someone poor is sure to get the blame."

As I set out that morning into a thick mist, I reflected on the thirty-odd individuals whom the Camino had brought together the night before, people gathered more or less at random and moved by no single faith or purpose. What modern day pilgrims had in common was just the fact of the Camino, the instructions in their guidebooks, the lines on their maps, and the yellow arrows painted on the rocks and trees.

The sun was soon starting to burn off the mist. I felt comfortable by now finding my way in mist or rain, even if occasionally my thoughts drifted too much into the clouds and I missed a turning. People were unfailingly helpful to pilgrims and seldom too busy to set them straight, perhaps because most, if not as Catholics then simply as Spaniards, would have it in their minds that they too, at some point in their lives, would be setting out with a rucksack to walk to Compostela.

As for the rest of us, what had once been referred to as a river of faith, had more recently being styled *"la ruta de la terapía."* And this too had a precedent in the Middle Ages in ships that were no longer useful for any other purpose having once been used to accommodate the disturbed. When filled to capacity, the vessel was allowed to set sail, but only to be abandoned by its crew once it was on the high seas, and henceforth left to the mercy of the wind and the waves. Such a vessel, in the Middle Ages, had given rise to the term Ship of Fools.

It was once again a Sunday and the main plaza of Belorado, at midday, was occupied by groups of men in dark suits waiting until the last moment before making their way to mass. Standing out above all of them was Park, who was beaming, having just found out that he would be allowed to stay in the monastery of Silos, where the monks had achieved world-wide renown by bringing out a recording of their Gregorian chants.

Sunday mornings were when I called home. When I had done so, we celebrated Park's good news with a *café con leche.* Having fallen somewhat behind the rest of us on account of his feet, Park confessed he had twice been forced to take a taxi, for which he professed himself contrite.

"But I'll make up for it, brother. I know now what I did wrong."

From various points about the plaza came the insistent ringing of church bells. His big mistake, according to Park, had been to arrive in Spain prepared physically to do the Camino, but not spiritually.

"Your rucksack was too heavy and your boots were too tight," I reminded him.

"That's just the point, brother. I was too proud. I was too sure of myself. I left nothing to God. What happened was all for my own good."

The notion that proof for our most strongly held beliefs can always be found if we look hard enough, was hardly new to me. The faith of pilgrims in the past had been strengthened by viewing this or that part of a saint, a drop of milk from the breast of the Virgin, crumbs from the Last Supper, a chip of stone from the Gates of Paradise, a sliver of wood from the cradle that Joseph had carved for the Niño Jesús. As for Park, the convert, who was more Catholic than the Pope, even his blistered feet could be viewed as a boon, and as proof that God loves us, and there was still a part of me that envied him this.

The refuge in Tosantos, the most "pure" on the entire Camino according to Paolo, was in the care of a monastic order. Once again we would sleep on the floor, this time in small rooms in what had once been the house of the village priest. The monk in charge of supper explained that he cooked more or less the same dish every night for a period of two weeks, after which another monk, with another dish, took over for two weeks.

We were joined at the table for the first time that evening by an elderly Italian couple, Giovanni and Sofia. They related, in a mixture of Italian and Spanish, how they were walking the Camino for the second time, some thirty years after the first, as a way of marking Giovanni's retirement. Until now they had gone off to mass each evening, and they were the only pilgrims I had so far encountered who had come equipped with their own sheets and pillowcases.

After the meal the monk invited us to attend a small service in the "chapel." What he called the chapel was a small garret room, carpeted, with a bench built into one wall, a simple altar lit by candles, and a stained glass window. We ourselves, the monk then gave us to understand, would be performing the service, each contributing in his or her own language.

"This seems very odd," Angelika whispered. "It makes my hairs stand on end."

Translations of a Bible passage chosen by the monk were passed out. There were, on that evening, six readings, in six different languages. When it was my turn to read, I did so slowly and clearly, finding it odd indeed to hear again, after so long, these words which had once been so familiar.

Next each of us was given a scrap of paper, a reflection on the Camino left behind by a previous pilgrim. Some spoke of their fatigue, some of their joy, and some had written poems. The reading of those notes in a cathedral would simply have been swallowed up by the vastness, but there within the stark confines of that attic the thoughts expressed by those unknown pilgrims brought more than one of us to the brink of tears.

Rita, the Dutch pilgrim, had turned up earlier and, declining any food, had instead gone directly to the dormitory, unrolled her sleeping bag, crawled into it, and pulled a blanket over her head. Before climbing into her own sleeping bag for the night, Angelika knelt down beside the Dutch woman's mat to listen for the sound of breathing.

"So," Angelika reported, "she is not yet a corpse. We can all, I think, sleep in peace until the snoring starts."

◆

The disciple of Santo Domingo de la Calzada was San Juan de Ortega, who carried on easing the way for pilgrims and who, after his death, became celebrated for miracles worked on behalf of childless women. No less a person than Isabel la Católica, the most famous of all Spanish queens, wishing to bear her husband King Ferdinand a son and heir, was said to have visited the tomb of this saint in order to pass about her waist the miraculous *cinta de San Juan de Ortega*, the tape or band which it was believed would bring about the end which she desired.

Her prayers to the saint having been said, the queen asked to view the holy remains. Although the corpse had not been disturbed since its interment, the clerics could hardly refuse such a powerful personage. The lid of the tomb was lifted, and from it appeared a great swarm of white bees. All the while that the uncorrupted body was being viewed, the bees circled beneath the roof of the crypt. Once the lid had been replaced they returned through a small hole which had hitherto gone unnoticed.

Thus was the original belief strengthened, and henceforth any sighting of one of the bees was a matter for celebration. For the faithful, the bees became "*las almas de los no nacidos*," the souls of children not yet born.

If the bees were souls awaiting their destiny, which were one day to be born into the world as mortals, they were also the guardians of the tomb. The renown of the saint having spread, a plan was hatched to transfer the sarcophagus from the chapel of the monastery in which it was housed to a larger and a grander church, a plan foiled by the fierceness of the bees and, according to the tale afterwards told, by their loyalty to the saint with whom they shared a home.

◆

The night had been cold, and when I awoke the surrounding hills were covered with a fine dusting of snow. The monk was already in the kitchen preparing coffee and slicing bread, and he reminded me, as I was laying the table for breakfast, to leave a note behind, in whatever language I wished, for subsequent pilgrims to read out over the coming twenty days, by which time I ought to have reached Compostela and my note could be retired.

The only other early risers that morning were Giovanni and Sophia. It was a fine thing, we agreed, that the notes left behind should be kept for just so long, thus producing not an ever-growing archive of reflections, which would soon become overwhelming, but a body of thought and of impressions which was ever-changing, a perpetual work-in-progress.

At the top of the first hill of the day, the snow crunched beneath my boots. The sun, however, had already broken through the clouds, and the path by which I descended was soon running with water. In my own note I had simply expressed the hope that the Camino might somehow survive amongst the *carreteras*, the Way amongst the highways.

The place now called San Juan de Ortega, Saint John of the Nettles, was a small hamlet with a very large church. In the adjacent bar, where I stopped for a sandwich, I was told that I had arrived some three weeks too late to witness a miracle. The church had been designed by its sainted architect so that, at the two equinoxes, the light of the setting sun illuminated, within the building, a scene set in stone of the Annunciation.

And how was it a miracle, I inquired, that nature should repeat itself year after year?

"Come back one day and see for yourself," a woman seated at the bar suggested, "before you decide."

Some six kilometres further on was the village of Atapuerco, just outside of which was an archaeological site, apparently of some importance. A chain link fence surrounded the site, and the gates were secured with a padlock. As I was peering through the fence, uncertain as to what I might see, a farmer with a wheelbarrow full of manure paused in order to let me know that nothing would be happening there again until the summer.

"The gentlemen who work here don't use shovels," he added. "They use spoons, and what they dig up in a day wouldn't even fill this barrow. They don't exactly tire themselves out."

"That sounds to me like a fine sort of job to have."

"That's what I say as well. And the easier the work, the more it pays."

The refuge at Atapuerco had not long since served as some manner of farm building and even now provided only the most basic of human accommodation. The temperature was once more dropping, but a quick forage through the village yielded an armful of firewood for the wood-burning stove, all that was needed to turn a cold and draughty structure into something a great deal more cosy.

By the time I had taken a shower, two more pilgrims had arrived and were warming their hands at the stove. They were a couple from Valladolid and had read that this refuge still smelled of animals, so had intended to stay at the adjacent hotel, but then they had noticed smoke coming from the chimney of the refuge and decided to investigate.

The man was called Martín, and his wife, Marisol.

"I'm surprised that you knew how to light the stove," the man said.

"Most foreigners, when they come to Spain, are completely helpless. We must have dinner together tonight."

"That's no way to invite someone," his wife reproached him.

I whiled away what remained of the afternoon writing postcards. Of those with whom I had become accustomed to spending this dead time, only Lawrence and Declan turned up that afternoon. The rest had chosen to sleep in the monastery at San Juan de Ortega..

"Give me a barn any day," Lawrence proclaimed. "I'm not the sort to be locked up at ten o'clock at night in a house of worship."

Declan's clock was ticking down. He didn't know, he admitted, how he was going to be able to face Dublin again so soon, and just when he was starting to get the hang of stringing together a few words of Spanish.

"I'm not saying that I can speak it, mind. It's early days for that. As for understanding what people are saying..." Declan shrugged. "The thing about a foreign language is that no one waits for you to figure out what one sentence means before they go on to the next one."

I left them later deep in discussion in the hotel bar and set off to join Martín and Marisol at the restaurant they had picked out of their guide book. I agreed that Martín should order for all of us. The Camino presented an excellent opportunity, Martín pontificated, to sample *platos regionales*, the dishes of the regions through which we were walking.

"My husband should have been a priest," Marisol said fondly. "Next to eating, he likes nothing better than to preach."

"Ask Roberto," Martín protested. "Is it true or not, Roberto, that most foreigners, when they come to Spain, order only dishes that they already know?"

Before I could work out a reply, Marisol had already done so.

"Most foreigners, when they come to Spain, don't come for a lecture on gastronomy."

Whoever was right about foreigners in Spain, we ate very well indeed, and far into the night. Even Lawrence, for once, was tucked up in bed by the time that I fell, exhausted, into mine.

HEROES OF SPAIN

✝

*Not seeing the truth, they knocked
at the door of fables.*

Hafiz

Any human history, it has been said, ought also to be a history of the mythology by means of which those living in a particular time and place understood the world about them. What stories were told, by whom and to what purpose, and how did those stories evolve? The account given by history is after all but the latest edition of what has already been told many times in many different ways, and with what authority can any history so far concocted claim to be the final version?

The figure of Santiago, a warrior on horseback, and the hero and saviour of Spain, first surfaced when the Reconquest was already well advanced. Not far from the city of Logroño is the village of Clavijo, and it was there that a battle was said to have been fought which present-day historians doubt ever actually occurred. What did happen, on the other hand, and what was merely imagined to have occurred, might at certain points in our human history produce scarcely distinguishable results.

According to the story, the lands of Asturias had for some time been protected from the depredations of the Moors by the payment of a shameful tribute, namely the annual surrender of a hundred maidens for use in their harems. Wishing to obliterate this stain on Spain, the Apostle appeared in a dream to the Christian king of Asturias and offered his help in a battle against the Moors if the king would only dare to undertake it. Perhaps it was no accident that the words of the saint to the king of Asturias echoed those with which Charlemagne, it was already believed, had been stirred to aid the Spanish cause.

The ensuing battle began badly, and the enemy was before long in the ascendancy. Then a cloud appeared in the sky, and in the cloud could be seen an unknown horseman, mounted on a white steed, brandishing a silver sword in one hand and holding in the other a banner bearing the sign of the cross. Thus was born, or invented, Santiago Matamoros, Saint James the Moorslayer, and in vain did the Mohammedans call upon their own champion, their own esteemed dead hero for aid.

The Apostle, following the alleged battle of Clavijo, was said to have been rewarded with a horseman's share of the booty. Following the appearance of the *story* of the alleged Battle of Clavijo, a corn and wine tax was levied on all the lands of Spain free of Moorish rule, the so-called *Voto de Santiago*, a vow, a gift, a tax in kind, ear-marked for the shrine of the Apostle, for its upkeep and future aggrandizement.

◆

There was no need to delay my own departure in order to set off from Atapuerca in the company of Martín and Marisol. Although not normally early risers, neither were they accustomed to the exertion of walking, and thus they had to start with the first light in order to complete even the short distances that they covered each day.

Martín, once we had picked up the path again, began relating a long joke about George W. Bush, interrupting himself every now and again to explain some expression which he thought that most foreigners who came to Spain would fail to understand. The gist of the joke was that, as president, Bush was prepared to impose the right to life on unborn foetuses and the terminally ill, while, as governor of Texas, he had been only too ready to execute helpless prisoners, who may or may not have been guilty as charged.

We paused after a time to watch the sunrise. He himself had once seemed destined for politics, Martín recalled. He had been a lawyer until his mid-forties, and active in politics during the first two elections after the death of Franco, following which a serious heart attack had stopped him in his tracks.

"Who would have guessed," he reflected, "that the hardest thing in life would be to take things easier."

He no longer practiced law, as he found it impossible to do so in a calm and rational way. Practicing law was like playing a competitive sport, there was no point to it unless you were prepared to do your very best in order to win. In the end he had hit upon a compromise: he now wrote articles for law journals.

The conversation then turned back to food. According to his guidebook, there was a *cafetería* on the way to Burgos, which would be our next port of call, that specialized in *torrijas*, which he considered a great delicacy. As we continued, he described in painstaking detail just how these ought to be made, adding that they were best eaten drenched in a sweet syrup.

"Naturally they're not good for him," said Marisol.

"But that fails to take into account all this walking," Martín rebutted.

I didn't have the heart to tell him that I had in fact eaten these before, not in Spain but as a child growing up in Virginia, where we had drenched them with a mock maple syrup and called them French toast.

The walk into Burgos through its suburbs was long and tedious, with nothing to distinguish these outskirts from those of any other Spanish city of a similar size, apart from a distant view of the cathedral towers. So much bustle and noise was disconcerting after days in the countryside, and it was a relief to arrive at the older quarter of the city with its upstairs *fondas* and *pensiones*, its dark narrow streets and ubiquitous small *tiendas* offering everything from sausages to second-hand books, from belts and ladies' handbags to the full panoply of religious paraphernalia, such as statuary, paintings, missals, rosary beads, postcards, and much else which I could not have named.

I emptied my pockets in the tiny, windowless room of a *pensión*, then stepped into the shower just as I was. I washed out each item of clothing as I removed it, using a nail brush on any encrusted mud before stepping on the garments in the bottom of the shower, as if treading grapes.

Dressed in clean but wrinkled clothing dredged from the bottom of my rucksack, I made my way to the cathedral to secure that day's *sello*, another day and another stamp in my pilgrim passport as proof that the person who bore it had negotiated the Camino in a manner consistent with his having done so under his own steam. Wearing trainers rather than boots, and without the weight of a rucksack on my back, I felt lighter than air.

The cathedral bells were ringing continuously as I arrived, and I soon found out why. Just when I had been setting out into the Pyrenées, a pope was being buried, and now, that very afternoon, in Rome, a new pope had been elected. The man chosen was the German, Ratzinger, of whom some German pilgrims eating ice cream cones on the cathedral steps remarked, sarcastically, that he was the perfect choice, just the man to lead the Church back into the Middle Ages.

A well-dressed woman walking past with a small dog on a lead stared at us fiercely. Had she understood the remark? Was she offended by the cut-off shorts of the German women? By the ice creams? This was a day, after all, which many would regard not just as a date in history, but also as an event in their own lives.

◆

The story of Rodrigo Díaz de Vivar, El Cid, El Campeador, the Battler, could be said both to begin and to end in the city of Burgos. Born not far from the city in the eleventh century, the Cid Campeador was born into conflict. War ebbed and flowed about him, loyalties were ever-shifting, and the fortunes of no man, least of all of a warrior, were ever certain. Thus the *Poema de Mío Cid*, with regard to its hero, commences with a lament that such a good vassal should not have been blessed with an equally good lord.

Although of proven prowess on the battlefield, El Campeador found himself falling foul of meddlers at court. Unjustly banished from his homeland, he was denied lodging in Burgos (where there would one day be statues and a plaza to honour him) and not even allowed to buy food.

At a loss as to what to do, the Cid Ruy Díaz received his answer in a dream in which the angel Gabriel appeared.

"Ride out, good Cid Campeador," the angel bade him. "The time has never been more propitious, and you will always meet with success."

So, empowered by his dream, the Cid became an outcast, a mercenary, attacking Christians as well as Moors, fighting first for one side and then for the other for the booty that it brought him. Great were the triumphs, the poem continues, and great were the vicissitudes of this hero, whose vacillations, as he was forced time and again to change sides, perhaps reflected the suspicion voiced at the time that it was the sins of the Christians, and above all their chronic disunity, which best accounted for the apparently superior strength of their enemies.

◆

Angelika turned up at the cathedral that evening at precisely the agreed time. As we began our tour, however, I noticed that she was limping.

"I think it is only nothing," she insisted. "I am walking too long, it may be, without resting."

We began by following the numbers, directed by arrows, which it was now our second nature to follow. We passed from chapel to chapel, but it was all the same, Angelika complained, nothing but images of suffering.

"Always I am asking why. Is it to scare people?"

"Suffering exists," I replied, for the sake of argument. "Don't you read about it every day, even in Switzerland, in the newspapers?"

"Not much. I read newspapers for knowing what films are showing."

We stood at last before the tomb of El Cid. Not until the twentieth century had the Bishop of Burgos been able to secure the body of El Campeador for reburial within the cathedral. The attention of my companion, however, had been drawn elsewhere, to a painting on the wall of the Last Supper.

"Look at the one beside Christ!" she exclaimed, suddenly enthusiastic. "Can't you see that it's a woman?"

"It would certainly make a good story."

"Yes, but I am asking you to look and tell me is it true."

Was it true? Had Mary Magdalene been present at the Last Supper? Was she the wife of Christ, and had she been the mother of his children? Or was it simply that this made for a better story, for our own times, than did the original?

"But I am asking you," Angelika persisted. "Use your eyes. Why is there one disciple that has no beard?"

Within the cathedral was a statue believed to have been copied from the actual body of Christ. The figure was all the more realistic for being covered in human skin. It was said in the past to have bled and perspired, and to have needed its beard and nails trimmed every eight days.

"Shall we find out where they keep it?" I asked Angelika. "Or go and have a coffee?"

"Go and have a coffee."

That was the evening when we would be bidding farewell to Declan. Burgos, we had heard, was famous for its *tapas* bars, and Martín was clearly pleased to have been asked to be our guide.

"Tell your friends that they must eat and drink slowly. This will not be a race, but an evening to be remembered."

We began in the quarter beside the cathedral. By the time that we reached the second bar, our numbers had risen to a dozen. Martín, as soon as he realized that Angelika spoke a little Spanish, commenced telling her, with many asides, the joke about George W. Bush.

"Normally my husband is shy," Marisol confided. "But with foreigners he loses all his inhibitions."

"I didn't realize that it was possible," I said, "for a lawyer to be shy."

"Oh yes, even an actor can be shy. And the shyer the person is, the more carefully he will prepare."

We were spread out along the counter. Marisol, short and compact, was perched on a stool with her legs tucked under her. Now and again she took a sip from a glass of white wine, half of which she left behind each time we moved on. She didn't need to drink to feel happy, she explained, only to be in the company of others who were enjoying themselves.

"Above all it makes me happy to see my husband happy. I'm like the *camaleón*, I take the colour of those around me."

His previous attempt having fallen flat, Martín was now telling Angelika a joke about Burgos, and Angelika was frowning with concentration as she strained to understand. Burgos had two "*estaciones*," the joke went, winter and the train station, and catching on to the joke depended on knowing that the word "*estación*," in Spanish, meant both station and season.

In the third bar, a small one into which nearly a score of pilgrims managed to crowd, Declan made a speech. He would never forget either the experiences which he had had on the Camino, or those with whom he had shared them. He would have liked to be able to carry on, now that he was getting the hang of things, but a man had to do, once his hair began to fall out, what a man had to do.

Marisol turned to me, but not to ask for a translation. Why, she wanted to know, if Declan was returning to Ireland to marry the woman that he loved, did he seem so sad?

"No," I prevaricated, "not sad, not really. Just thoughtful."

◆

Artists are never far behind the storytellers. What is first told in stories is then illustrated in the images which every society produces and in which it inevitably comes to see itself reflected. This is nothing new, nor has it been superseded, for although the images may constantly change, the idolatry does not.

The image of Santiago Matamoros, still in view the length of the Camino and elsewhere, is of an armed warrior mounted on a rearing horse, waving a sword, holding a cross, and trampling underfoot the turbaned enemy. In the New World, where Indians were substituted for Moors, the image became that of Santiago Mataindios. Back on the peninsula, in the propaganda of the Spanish Civil War, when godless communists were seen by some to be the threat, Santiago Matamoros assumed the guise of Santiago Matarojos.

Where it was possible to remove the trampled figures of the enemy, a less bellicose image was obtained, that of Santiago Caballero, the horseman saint. It was said that General Franco, when it was necessary to entertain his North African troops, ordered flowers strategically placed so that his guests need not look upon cowering and abject Moors.

Least warlike of all is the image of Santiago Peregrino. On foot and unarmed, wrapped in a cloak and carrying a staff, sporting a scallop shell on his hat, and often leaning into the wind, the Apostle is portrayed as a pilgrim en route to his own tomb. Illogical perhaps, but a good deal more politic.

◆

Beyond Burgos waited the Meseta, a vast tableland. Here, amongst other difficulties, warned an old Spanish guide book which Martín had shown us the night before, the pilgrim was likely to find little to distract him from his own thoughts. That worn, leather bound, and long out of date guide book, with its commonsense advice, was of much greater advantage to the pilgrim, Martín had argued, than was the Michelin map carried by his wife.

What first distracted me from my own thoughts on the road beyond Burgos was the sight of a stork nesting on top of the chimneys of a disused factory. As I stood gazing at the bird I became aware of someone coming up quickly behind me, a pilgrim of about my own age, who as he drew closer seemed to be on the verge of bursting into tears. I greeted him in Spanish, receiving a reply in English.

"Please excuse me, sir. I am Belgian. I have just begun today."

His name was Albert. He had arrived in Burgos by train only the night before. He peered up at the crane for a moment, but he was clearly in a hurry to move on.

"Yes, that is an extraordinary bird, but now I must continue. *A bientot.*"

"*Buen Camino.*"

Field after field of grain stretched before us, squared off by intersecting gravel roads, and it was these which the Camino itself was following, in a zigzag fashion. This, for someone not accustomed to the way-marking, must have proved confusing, for I suddenly realized that the Belgian had gone right past one of the turnings and was now headed off at full speed in the direction of a distant forest.

Rushing ahead to the turning, I called after him, hailing him at the top of my lungs until he at last looked back over his shoulder. I gestured, indicating where he had gone off the route, and it wasn't long before, with his long and relentless stride, he had once again eaten up the ground between us.

"I want to thank you, sir. That was very kind indeed."

"Wherever there's a crossroads, look for a shell or an arrow. Racing off in the wrong direction won't get you very far."

"Indeed it won't, sir. That's excellent advice. *A bientot.*"

"*Buen Camino.*"

Walking thirty kilometres over flat ground was by now little more than a stroll. At the refuge in Hontanas I found that Albert had arrived safely, had showered and shaved and was lying in his bunk reading a book which appeared to be a Bible.

The refuge was run out of a bar. The dormitories were above, the bar and a *comedor* below. That afternoon the bar was crowded and noisy, so I slipped into the empty dining room with a beer and my notebook, closing the door behind me. I was now nearing the mid-point of the Camino, by the route that I had chosen, and feeling ever more confident that there was nothing that the Camino could throw at me, short of an accident or a serious illness, that could prevent me from reaching the end. Nothing, after all, boosts the confidence as much as setting others straight.

I was still making my notes for the day when Angelika came into the dining room. She was hobbling badly, and looking anything but happy.

"My foot was very bad today," she reported. "Maybe you can look and tell me what is the cause."

She set down her beer on the table, pulled out a chair, dropped into it, and placed her bare foot in my lap. The tendon behind the ankle, the Achilles, was swollen, red, and hot to the touch.

"You see?" she said. "I am not myself making up any stories."

She had not thought to bring any medicines with her. She was accustomed to walking in the Alps, and had never experienced any difficulties. But the ankle, it then came out, was far from the only thing troubling her.

"I have had a phone message today already from Switzerland…"

She had spoken to me several times about her boyfriend, a man some fifteen years her senior, who had custody of his two children from a previous marriage and who had for some time been pestering her to move in with him. Now, it seemed, he was demanding that she make up her mind immediately.

"He says that he can no longer wait for me. He thinks that the Camino is only my excuse. Sometimes I am thinking what I could even want with such a man."

The tendonitis I could try to treat with an anti-inflammatory cream which I fetched from my rucksack, but the boyfriend was more complicated. Having read the cautions on the tube of ointment, I asked Angelika if she were pregnant.

"How could I be pregnant? He says that he has already enough children."

I squeezed out a little of the cream and rubbed it as gently as possible into the inflamed tissue. What a pity it would be if this bit of muscle, which had served her well so far, should now turn against her. Angelika slouched lower in her chair, took a long drink of her beer, and sighed as if she alone bore all the weight of the world on her thin shoulders.

There were many new faces in the dining room that evening, the faces of those who, like Albert, had begun their Camino that morning in Burgos. On the other hand we were without Declan and, for the moment, without Paolo, who would have considered that *albergue* too expensive, and without Park, who had taken a bus on from Burgos to Silos, to stay with the monks. Our make-shift family, the chance company of pilgrims to which we belonged, had thus been reduced and was under threat of being swamped by strangers.

I introduced Albert to the others, rather than condemning him to a solitary meal.

"You must excuse me," he apologized, unnecessarily, "because my English is not so good."

"No one will notice," Lawrence assured him. "Just remember to say, from time to time, 'I believe it's my round.'"

"Thank you, sir," Albert responded, with no variation in his hangdog look. "I will need to bear that in mind."

Their first day on the Meseta had left Martín and Marisol completely played out, and even when they did finally manage to drag themselves down to the dining room, they weren't yet ready for a meal. While Marisol attempted to trace out on her map the route of the next day's stage, Martín recounted for us how a notorious *hospitalero* in Burgos had once succeeded in poisoning hundreds of pilgrims in order to take possession of their goods, and committed over four hundred murders before he was eventually discovered and put to death with his own poison.

"Only my husband," Marisol interposed, "would think of telling such a story while people are eating."

"*Hombre advertido vale por dos*," Martín reposted.

"That sounds a pithy saying," said Lawrence. "What does it mean?"

"Forewarned is forearmed."

We left the couple still sitting in the *comedor*, still not having ordered their meal. Martín was engrossed in his treasured guidebook, Marisol was picking at a bowl of olives. Angelika, as we made our way up the stairs to the dormitory, remarked on what a great difference there was between husband and wife, Marisol being so sensible and Martín so impractical.

"Perhaps it's enough," I suggested, "for just one of them to be sensible."

"Then I am asking if they will not always have arguments."

"Perhaps they've learned how to argue. Do you understand what it means, in English, to pull your punches?"

Angelika frowned. She was walking more easily again, for the moment at least, but that was in sandals. What would be the case in the morning when she again laced up her boots?

"Maybe I have not yet found true love," she reflected. "To argue is for me very painful. So I am always thinking there are more fishes somewhere in the sea."

OLD STAGERS

✝

I beg you therefore,
while we are pilgrims in this world and soldiers on earth,
let us not build for ourselves houses to settle down in
but make tents we can leave at a moment's notice.

Saint John Chrysostom

Myths, wrote William James, are "authentic tidings of invisible beings." Like many other definitions, this acknowledges the paradoxical nature of myths. Myths have been defined as artful fictions, and useful falsehoods, suggesting that the bare facts of a matter are not always sufficient. The suggestion is that myths address what facts alone fail to explain, satisfying us in a way different from any mere recital of those facts.

We seek meaning beyond that which the available evidence can provide, we seek certainty where nature appears to offer only probability. What does not exist we have imagined, what we have not found we have created. Where coherence is wanting, we have imposed it. Facts may at times be counter-intuitive, myths can never be.

Where we err, it is on the side of order, unable to bear that life should be haphazard. We give shape in the world to what we afterwards fail to recognize as being suspiciously akin to our own wishes. We seek the help of powers which we have ourselves first envisioned as being helpful, we gird ourselves for battle against demons which we ourselves have placed in the world to thwart our progress.

We are humankind. We are a work in progress, and still feeling our way. We look back anxiously over our shoulders, we gaze up into the heavens in awe. We are the children of our demons as well as of our gods: we will go to whatever length necessary sooner than face being on this earth on our own, and mere creatures of a day.

A miracle, according to Saint Augustine, was an incomprehensible or uncommon event, which, by overwhelming human reason, strengthened our faith. Miracles, beginning with the Passion of Christ and its aftermath, were breaks in the logic of the world, but at the same time miracles were not without a logic of their own. The course of a saint's life on earth and the nature of his martyrdom, according to that logic, determined just what manner of help that saint could be called upon to render, and thus was the torment and often gruesome death of a saint transformed into a balm for the afflictions of the living.

The Apostle, whilst first traversing the wilds of Spain, was himself said to have known hardship, doubt, and despair. For the disciple of Christ and future saint, the natural was the supernatural, and he would hardly have been surprised to receive, when at his lowest ebb, a visit from the Virgin Mary, who, in order to restore his spirits, left with him with an image of herself mounted on a column, the image of a mother and child which would subsequently be venerated as Nuestra Señora del Pilar.

To whom then, centuries later, would a lone pilgrim who was starving and without funds for food choose to appeal, but to the saint who, in a similar place, had known similar travails? Having prayed to the Apostle before retiring, the famished pilgrim was granted a vision of Santiago that night as he slept, a vision in which he was being presented by the saint with a loaf of bread. The miracle, as afterwards recorded, wasn't in the dream, which might easily enough have been explained, but in what the pilgrim, when he awoke, found resting on the ground beside him.

◆

One of the new German pilgrims, a young student walking on her own, followed me from the dormitory in the dark carrying her rucksack, her sleeping bag, and her trousers. We began packing up in the corridor just as the first faint light of day was seeping back into the sky. The girl's name was Maika. The school holidays, she told me, had commenced only a few days previously and her friends back in Germany thought her mad to be going off by herself on a pilgrimage when anyone else their age would have preferred going to the beach.

"But I find most people my age to be silly, and they, I suppose, find me to be strange."

The bar downstairs was already dispensing *café con leche* and *tostadas*. As we were eating, Albert the Belgian appeared, wished us a good morning, complained that he had overslept, politely declined a coffee, and continued on towards the door to the street.

"*A bientot.*"

Albert had been in the bunk beneath Maika, and she was certain that she had heard him sobbing during the night. Not knowing whether he was in pain or having a nightmare, she hadn't been sure whether or not to wake anyone else.

"He seemed fine just now," I assured her. "That was probably the last we'll see of him all day."

"Do you think that he might be a penitent?"

"I'd find it hard to explain even why I'm here, much less what possesses anyone else."

The sun was just rising behind us as we began our own day's walk. Maika, who was little short of six feet tall and very thin, was pleasant company, and she spotted what I might otherwise have missed, a vixen trotting with her young across a rock-strewn field. She liked nature, and felt much more at home walking in a forest than she did dancing in a discothèque.

She must have learned, in the forests of Germany, not to be afraid of silence. Between one village and the next only our footfalls disturbed the tranquillity of the *campo*. Only when we stopped in a bar for a coffee and to use the toilets was our conversation resumed.

"May I ask you," Maika inquired, "what sort of work you do?"

"No sort of work," I replied, "not really. I write stories."

"And you don't find writing difficult?"

"Writing well is difficult, but I still wouldn't call it work."

She liked reading. She liked, in particular, Herman Hesse and expected from a book that it should contain more than it was possible to understand at any single period of the reader's life.

"You like getting your money's worth from a book?"

"Yes, you may say so. And always, in the fairy tales that I liked best when I was a child, there was someone who knew the way and who gave good advice."

I left her in a small street market shopping for a sunhat. A little further on the track began to climb, and I soon passed Giovanni and Sofia, whom I regularly passed several times each day, as they never stopped along the way for coffee or for a *tinto* or for *bocadillos*.

"*¡Hola, Roberto! Tan rapido como siempre.*"

The hills of Scotland had left me well prepared. I leaned forward, matching my pace to the steepness of the path as it rose, allowing the contours of the landscape to dictate my pace. It was up to the walker to find the rhythm of the hill, the ideal tempo being one which brought him to the summit no more than mildly fatigued, and only a little out of breath so he could enjoy the sensation, for those few moments before beginning to descend, of being the master of all he surveyed.

Whatever the nature of her own pilgrimage, Sheila the energy worker seemed to have no trouble at all talking her way into refuges and, once installed, making herself completely at home. I encountered her next in the courtyard of the *albergue* at Boadilla del Camino, seated with a sketchpad propped open in her lap and an empty beer mug resting on the ground beside her.

"I thought that you'd likely fetch up here," she greeted me. "However much you might deny the hidden currents of the earth, that doesn't disconnect you from them."

She asked then what changes I had noticed in myself. Just the ones that you would expect, I replied. I was no longer aware of either the rucksack on my back, or of my boots, nor did I any longer worry about losing my way. I now, in short, felt completely at home on the Camino.

"Just be careful," Sheila warned. "You might end up not feeling at home again anywhere else afterwards."

I asked her if she had run into Park. Not lately, Sheila said, and Park was hard to miss. She reached down into her carry-all and withdrew a portfolio. The pilgrim in the sketch which she handed over, although facing away, was clearly Park, captured in the process of packing his rucksack.

"*Un sitio para cada cosa*," the caption read, "*y cada cosa en su sitio*."

A place for everything and everything in its place. I asked her then what had given her the idea of presenting her sketches in this fashion, and she admitted that she was merely following the example of Francisco Goya, who had produced a number of ironically titled sketches intended to illustrate the many absurdities of his own times.

"So you consider the Camino to be absurd?" I queried, surprised.

"The Camino is what it is. The absurdity lies elsewhere."

After I had showered, washed my clothes and hung them out to dry, she asked me to come with her to look at a *rollo*. This was a wayside cross originally used for marking boundaries, and on which oaths had once been sworn. While clearly powerful as a symbol, the cross also served to channel energy, according to Sheila, especially when planted in the earth.

"It operates similarly to a lightning rod. And crosses were venerated long before they were used for crucifixions. It's the same old story, what ancient peoples already knew has since had to be reinvented."

"And what makes you so sure of all this? Were you a Druid once yourself?"

"That reminds me," was her only reply.

Like a magician pulling a rabbit out of a hat, she withdrew another sketch from her portfolio. Although she had again contrived not to show the pilgrim's face, there could be no doubt as to who it was. She must have done it in Logroño, in the Bar Picasso, as it showed me bent over a copy of *Marca*, the Spanish sports newspaper, overlooked in turn by the bar's pet parrot.

And the caption?

El Camino acabará por repararte.
The Camino will end up repairing you.

◆

Even when most alone on the road, a pilgrim was never alone in his quest. It happened that a group of pilgrims setting out on horseback from France made a pact of mutual assistance, as was customary at the time, but with one of their number, a pilgrim called Lotario, refusing to join in the oath. Once the party had crossed into Spain, one of its members fell ill, and his condition worsened until it was clear that he could no longer continue. Despite their oath, his companions chose to abandon their stricken companion and leave him to his fate, all apart from Lotario, who, despite having been no party to the oath, elected to remain behind.

The end came on a mountain, where the soul of the ailing pilgrim, in the words of the *Codex*, went out of this worthless world. Alone on a mountain top with a corpse, Lotario called fervently on the Apostle for help, upon which the Soldier of God materialized, on horseback. Taking the corpse up into his arms the saint ordered Lotario to mount behind him. And as the pilgrimage was resumed not on the surface of the earth but over the road used by the saints, a journey of weeks was completed in a single night.

By sunrise the travellers had reached the Monte de Gozo, a hilltop overlooking the city towards which the pilgrims had been bound. A grave was dug there for his erstwhile companion, and Lotario was then free to continue on and start the accustomed vigil at the tomb of the Apostle. As for the others, their penance would be severe, and they would face many trials and tribulations before reaching the city of the saint and the goal which Lotario had achieved, not by means of any oath, false or otherwise, but through the goodness of his heart and the purity of his soul.

◆

The way beyond Boadilla was completely flat, dead straight, and all but featureless apart from a canal and the occasional chimney or bell tower which had been colonized by storks. I caught up with a woman who always walked her dog along the path of the Camino, she told me, in order to meet and chat with pilgrims. She accompanied me into the village in which she lived, pointing out the house of the priest, her sister-in-law's house, and the house of a man who had once visited London.

As the day was fine I took my lunch of bread, cheese, sausage, and olives, and sat in the sun, with my back against a low stone wall. The landscape about me was flat and near to featureless all the way to the horizon. High above the plain a dark swarm of birds was moving off, heading north, kept on course throughout their migration, science suggested, by the earth's magnetic field. It was obviously an error, I was reminded, to believe too little, to believe only in what one's own senses could discern.

And why not some other sort of energy beneath the surface of the earth, one upon which human beings could rely to keep them on their course? Her art, Sheila had told me the evening before, was neither high art, nor was it mere decoration, it was practical. Her sketches were intended as a guide, another sort of guide, a guide to the Camino for another sort of pilgrim.

Before hoisting my rucksack again I took out a chocolate bar to nibble on as I walked. So far as I had seen until now, it was *just* the walking that mattered, the simple act of walking, not the path or the crosses or the good will or the good offices of a long dead saint. It was the walking, day after day, in any sort weather. The complexity of modern life was thus reduced to just one simple, straightforward, recurring task, that of getting oneself from place to place by one's own efforts alone.

"You're still a novice," Sheila had told me in the *albergue*, in front of a log fire. "You're just getting going. You're not yet looking past the end of your own nose."

The priest in charge of the refuge at Carrión de los Condes called my attention to a sign on the wall announcing that a video would be shown that evening as an introduction to the town and to its spiritual dimension. As a further inducement for pilgrims to attend, wine and biscuits were to be served. Well-managed and industrious, the town had been lauded in the *Codex*, in what served as the earliest of the pilgrim guidebooks.

Present day guidebooks warned the pilgrim to stock up on food here on account of the long and desolate stretches of Meseta which lay beyond. By the evening, shopping bags full of groceries from a nearby *supermercado* littered the dormitory.

Angelika declared she wasn't interested in the "spiritual dimension" of the town, nor was she tempted by the offer of a free glass of wine. If the wine was free, she predicted, it would be ordinary wine, and served cold, straight out of the refrigerator.

"I will do something more useful. I will look for where I can send my emails and then maybe I will wash my hair if there are not in the shower already other kinds of hairs."

Others had their own excuses, which left only the Italians, Giovanni and Sofia, Albert the sad Belgian, and Maika, the long-legged student from Düsseldorf. The video showed the various religious images of the town as they were being carried in procession through the streets during *Semana Santa*. Here was one more town, Carrión de los Condes, in the growing list of towns which but for the pilgrimage we would never have heard of, but which now we would never forget.

The "Swiss Miss," Lawrence called Angelika, and that night she was fuming. She had spent an hour on a computer in a bar composing an e-mail only to have the line drop so that she wasn't able to send it. Such things always happened in Spain, she raged, because the Spanish never finished anything. There was always something that hadn't been attached right or that didn't work properly, and thus whatever the Spanish attempted, in her opinion, ended up being nothing but a big waste of time.

"Now there's a sweeping statement for you," Lawrence said. "Not that I would necessarily disagree."

"Not that the English are much better," Angelika added.

Nor was that all. She was irritated that Martín and Marisol had now fallen behind and were unlikely to catch up again, that it had been impossible to buy just a single tub of yogurt in the *supermercado*, and that she had been unable to sleep properly for the last three nights because of all the snoring in the dormitories. A daughter, I was thus given the opportunity to observe, could also be tedious.

◆

The sixteenth of the miracles performed by Saint James, as listed in the *Codex*, involved a French soldier who, while making the pilgrimage to Compostela, came to the aid of a female pilgrim he found walking on her own and burdened with a sack. To her relief, he offered to transport the sack for her on his horse. Continuing on, the same soldier came upon a beggar walking the Camino with the aid of a stick, and again the soldier's heart was moved. He at once dismounted, allowing the invalid to ride while he himself continued on foot with the woman's sack hung round his neck and the stick of the cripple clutched in his hand.

The sun was hot and the journey wearisome, and the soldier, before reaching the city of the blessed James, fell ill. Taking into account the many ways that he had offended in the past, the soldier endured his discomforts calmly out of love for the Apostle, and so at last he arrived at the place he had sought. Having first prayed before the tomb, he then found lodging in the city and lay down on the narrow bed provided him, completely exhausted by his malady. Recognizing that death was near, the soldier wished to prepare himself to meet it, but was at first prevented from doing so by the oppressive presence of a band of dark spirits.

The demons made it their business to torment the dying soldier, some plucking at his tongue, others closing his eyes, still others twisting and contorting his body against his will, until at last Saint James himself entered the room. In his left hand the Apostle held the sack which the soldier had borne for another on the road and in his right hand the staff of the beggar for whom the soldier had given up his horse, and these were the weapons with which the saint, in his fury, attacked the demons that were gathered there and drove them from the room.

Having regained his speech and reassumed control over his body, the pilgrim-soldier could now confess and receive the viaticum of Holy Communion, and so come to rest, as the *Codex* relates, with a good end to his life. And what happier conclusion for a believer, for whom death was but the threshold of a better world, than to know that he was passing through that portal cleansed of his sins?

◆

While Angelika's rucksack and boots were still at the foot of her bunk the following morning, the bunk itself was empty. Not having found her in the corridor or the toilets, I located her finally curled up on a sofa in the reception room of the refuge, where she had gone during the night in order to escape the noise of the dormitory.

She stuck out her foot so that I could treat it. People who snored (and I myself was one of the worst offenders) should be made to sleep out in the street, in her opinion, either that or else be suffocated.

"Of course I do not really mean that," she added, not very convincingly.

The medicine which I had been applying eased the inflammation and brought the swelling down, but each day's walk undid all the good of the treatment. Although she was game enough, and certainly stubborn, her condition was unlikely to improve on its own, and it was still a long way to Compostela.

Music, meanwhile, had begun to blare throughout the refuge.

"Can you tell me please," Angelika moaned, "what is that?"

"It's Pachobel's *Canon*."

"I mean, why does it have to play so early?"

"To punish those who didn't watch the priest's video yesterday."

Not far beyond the town, I came upon a curious individual whom I had noticed for the first time the evening before in the refuge. He was elderly and quite shabby, with more of the appearance of a vagabond than of a pilgrim. As I approached the picnic table at which he was sitting, he began blowing a shrill whistle, and it crossed my mind that, in addition to being a tramp, he might also be mentally disturbed.

"*Hola, buenos días,*" I greeted him.

"*Muy buenos, caballero.*"

His breakfast was spread out over the table before him. There was some dirty looking cheese, olives, a bruised tomato and a wedge of hard bread that he might well have been handed at the back door of a restaurant.

I asked him for how long he had been walking the Camino.

"Ever since I can remember, *gracias a Dios.*"

Pressed by him to share his breakfast, I selected an olive, replacing it with a handful of dates. Without the Camino to guide his steps, the old man said, he would long since have become lost in the world. Without the Camino he would not have had a roof over his head, or a warm bed at night, or proper food to eat.

"And sometimes, *caballero*, even a little sip of wine…"

He broke off and snatched up his whistle. Maika was now in view on the path and the old man began blowing the whistle again frantically, until, seeing that Maika was becoming alarmed, I asked him to stop.

"She's only a girl," I said. "Can't you see that you're frightening her?"

"Frighten her, *caballero?* Why would I want to do that? I watched her getting undressed last night…"

He leaned towards me across the table, wishing to share a confidence.

"I saw it all, and that's the truth. And then I lay awake the whole night, watching over her in her sleep."

The village of Terradillos de los Templarios, having once been owned by the Knights Templars, was associated in its early history with Jacques

Demolay, there known as Jacobo de Molay, and was the setting for an esoteric version of the legend of the hen that laid the golden egg. The fondness of the Templars for gold, according to the accusations later levelled against the order, had led them not only to mine for that substance but also to seek for it by means of alchemy.

The day had turned wet, and there was already a wood fire blazing in the *comedor* of the *albergue* at Terradillos. Having secured a bed for the night, I joined Giovanni and Sofia, who were drinking tea at a table near the fire. Rain and early darkness made for a more sombre mood than usual.

"We were speaking of Park today," Giovanni told me. "What a shame if we never meet up with him again."

"We miss his smile," Sofia said. "He reminds us of a friendly Buddha."

The by now familiar sound of a shrill whistle reached us from the courtyard. I didn't need to voice my own suspicions about the old man, as Giovanni and Sofia had encountered him the evening before, at mass, where something in the priest's homily had reduced the old man to tears.

"We suspect," Giovanni added, lowering his voice, "that the poor man's mind might not be quite sound."

"Of course we are not doctors," Sofia said.

"Nevertheless," said Giovanni, "we have eyes."

As luck would have it this was one of the few refuges in which men and women slept in separate dormitories. I found the old man unpacking his rucksack onto the bed beside my own, laying out a seemingly endless number of small plastic bags the contents of which could only be guessed at. He studied the bags, shuffled them about a bit, and then started replacing them from whence they had come.

"I don't want to take up any more space than I'm entitled to," he explained.

That evening as usual I sat with Angelika, each of us bent over our notebooks with our backs to the others until that day's entries had been completed. After our meal had been concluded, we took a turn around the village and I told her, once we were alone, about the old man, leaving it to her to decide whether anything about this ought to be said to Maika.

"Yes," she said thoughtfully, for all the world like a child pleased to have been given an adult's job to do. "I will need to consider what is required to be done."

The sky was clearing, and beyond the last streetlight of the village we could view, above the plain of the Meseta another even vaster landscape, an apparently infinite expanse of stars.

"So tonight," Angelika reflected, "we will for once hear no men snoring. And that madman will be watching over *your* sleep."

◆

A certain Italian nobleman, an inveterate sinner who ignored both the wrath of God and the justice of men, bore on his conscience many heinous crimes which he had for a long time refused to confess. When finally his fear of the afterlife led to his sins being acknowledged, the priest who heard his confession, rather than impose a penance himself, ordered the penitent to make a list of all those deeds of which he was ashamed and to carry this list with him to the city of Saint James, there to implore the help of the blessed Apostle.

So it transpired that after an arduous journey the noble pilgrim arrived at the threshold of the cathedral bearing a *scedula*, a scroll containing all of those deeds for which he had come to seek absolution. Being sincerely repentant, and having with many tearful sobs begged for forgiveness from God and from the Apostle, the exhausted penitent then placed the document detailing his misdeeds upon the altar at the first hour of the saint's feast day, thus assuring that it would be found by the bishop when he arrived to say the morning mass.

As it was desired, so it occured. The bishop, finding a document awaiting him at the altar, at once broke the seal and unrolled the scroll which, to his amazement, he found to be blank. The parchment was unstained, as if no letters had ever been written upon it, as if none of the crimes to which the sinner had confessed had ever been committed. He who had borne the *scedula* was later called forward by the bishop, before the multitude that that morning crowded the cathedral.

"No further penance," the bishop declared, "is necessary. This parchment gives clear proof that your crimes have already been forgiven."

And thus was it clearly demonstrated for all to see that he who was truly penitent, and who arrived at the shrine of Saint James prepared to lay bare his heart, would find that the burden on his soul had been lifted, by the grace of the Apostle, and the slate of his sins wiped clean.

◆

I awoke much earlier than usual to find the dormitory flooded with light. The sky had cleared, there was a full moon, and I was suddenly anxious to be on my way. I dressed, packed my rucksack, left a note and the tube of anti-inflammatory for Angelika, and slipped out through the courtyard.

The way was first along a farm road. The sky was thick with stars, and the moon so bright as to cast shadows. Walking with only the lights above to guide me, I felt myself firmly placed, securely situated, and entirely safe in this country which was not my own, but to which the circumstances of my life had directed me.

With the dawn, a mist began rising off the land, which before long enveloped me. Once more it was a Sunday, my third so far on the Camino, and there was no sign of life on any of the isolated farms which I passed. Untroubled by my passing, none of the dogs of those places could be bothered to bark, a sure sign, I thought, of someone who was *en su sitio*, who was indisputably, at that moment, just where he belonged.

Some three hours of walking brought me to the town of Sahagún. In the heart of the town was a shop with its lights on, a *pastelería*, with the first of the day's pastries already arranged on a shelf. The woman in charge, after bringing what I had ordered, joined me with a coffee of her own. It was rare for her to have a customer this early, she said, although later in the day she would surely be rushed off her feet.

She was a widow. Her husband had been the baker, but now it was her son-in-law who did the baking, and she thanked God every day that her daughter had had the good sense to marry someone who didn't mind going to work in the dark.

We were interrupted by the sound of a whistle in the street outside. Thus alerted, the woman got up and went to the door of the shop, locking it from the inside.

"*Un sinvergüenza*," she explained.

A scoundrel, a rascal, a swine, a person who knew no shame. For years now the old tramp had been passing through the town every few months, headed first in one direction and then in the other.

"He has no home," the woman said, sitting back down. "He has no money and no sense. He goes about making disturbances. God ought to take better care of such unfortunates."

Far off a storm was sweeping across the Meseta. Lightning bolts flashed down from the clouds, distant thunder rumbled, a sheet of water swept from left to right before me across the plain, and then, just as suddenly as the storm had appeared, the sky ahead once more became clear blue. All in all a superb show had been presented, and completely free of charge.

Mass must have turned out in El Burgo Ranero, as the bar was packed with midday drinkers. Seated alone by the window, looking as gloomy as ever while he waited for the *comedor* to open, was Albert, the long-faced Belgian. He too had been to the mass, and so had missed the spectacle of the storm.

"This is an anniversary for me," he informed me without further preamble. "It's two months now since I lost my sister…"

The two beers which I had carried over from the bar entitled us to *tapas*, which that day were small dishes of chick peas and fat pork. For many years he and his sister had spoken of walking the Camino together, Albert continued, but year after year had passed and there had always been some reason why the walk had to be postponed.

"And now, you see, I must walk for us both."

The waitress signalled that the dining room was opening, and we moved across with our rucksacks. A bottle of wine and some bread were already on the table, and the first course of paella was at once set between us. The waitress wanted to know how far we were walking that day, so I told her we had come some thirty kilometres since setting out that morning, and still had more than a dozen to go to reach the refuge at Reliegos.

"¡Vaya! And on a day when everyone else is resting."

The second course was rabbit stew. Albert merely toyed with it, as he had done with the paella. Neither he nor his sister had ever married. They had never lived together as adults, but had resided in the same city and spent every weekend together doing things that they had both enjoyed.

"It was only natural, you understand. Our tastes were exactly alike, and not the same as anyone else's."

It was as though an entire life had been unfolded and spread out there on the table, amidst the crumbs of bread, the stray grains of saffron-coloured rice, and the wine stains. His sister, only a few months before, had suddenly become ill, and within weeks she had died.

"You never expect a thing like that. You think that there's nothing these days that can't be cured. Even the doctors, in her case, were taken by surprise."

No sooner had the remnants of the stew been cleared away, than portions of flan and cups of coffee were set before us. Unlike the other diners, who would sit chatting away happily for an hour or more after their meal, pilgrims, the waitress realized, would be anxious to be off.

"Right now I have no time for such things," she then remarked, "but one of these days I will surely do the Camino myself..."

This might have struck a little too close to home. Albert, fortunately, didn't ask me for a translation of what the waitress had said, and I saw no reason to volunteer one.

FORGIVE YOURSELF

✝

*Men are what they think; a man's destiny is
determined by his credence.*

Ralph Waldo Emerson

If the imagery of the saint has come to be altered over time, in accord
with new needs and new sensibilities, so too has the nature of the
Camino itself. The pilgrimage to Compostela was once a means to an
end, and for most a catalogue of hardships. The pilgrim setting off in the
springtime faced swollen rivers, suffocating heat and perishing thirst, and
would not expect to see his home again before the autumn.

Some may have set out fleeing famine or the Plague, but the concern
of most, and the true currency of a pilgrimage, was one's sins. Reaching
Santiago de Compostela wiped out a third of the pilgrim's sins, with
further indulgences being granted for visits to certain shrines en route.
Moreover, those who contrived to arrive in Compostela in a holy year, in
which the day dedicated to Saint James fell on a Sunday, might hope to
receive an absolute indulgence, a full remission of their sins, and so return
home, by the grace of the Apostle, with one foot already in Heaven.

Only a few now walk to Compostela bearing the burden of their sins,
fewer still, if any, to flee famine or a plague. There are, on the other hand,
those who leave behind lives blighted by poverty, illness, or grief. But
the majority? Rare indeed will be the pilgrim in his or her present day
incarnation who doesn't walk burdened by his or her excesses.

Whether in the twelfth or twenty-first centuries, the essence of the pilgrimage
remains what it has always been, which is the surrender of that to which one
is accustomed in the hope of encountering something better. The pilgrim
setting off must first dispense with the usual comforts and conveniences

of home, and this in itself can hardly fail to act on the pilgrim in ways which are unexpected. *El Camino siempre reserva sorpresas.* In the lore of the modern-day pilgrim, for whom the undertaking itself has become a protagonist, the Camino always has a surprise or two up its sleeve.

The pilgrim not already accustomed to doing so, must learn early on to travel light. The shelves in the *albergues* are heaped with goods of all sorts which over-burdened pilgrims have left behind, items which were not required on the journey. What one learns to do without, contemporary pilgrim narratives relate, is just what makes one stronger.

Pilgrims no longer cross poisonous rivers but they do cross motorways, skirt airports, and must wind their way through busy city streets. For the weary pilgrim, the careless pilgrim, the pilgrim made light-headed by the sun, the dangers are never far away. Wolves have merely been replaced by dogs, and highwaymen by light-fingered opportunists.

◆

Twelve hours on the road, during which time I had walked some forty-four kilometres across the plain, had left me none the worse for wear. I found Paolo in the kitchen of the refuge brewing up some *maté* for his breakfast, having been presented with the leaves by an Argentinean pilgrim. I accepted a glass for the sake of trying it, and so learned that *maté* was in fact less closely related to any sort of tea than it was to grass.

Having speared a slice of white bread on the end of a fork, Paolo set about toasting it, somewhat haphazardly, over the gas flame of the stove. As there was no butter in the refrigerator and no olive oil or marmalade in any of the cupboards, he squirted a little tomato paste onto the bread, the same tomato paste that he had used the evening before over his pasta.

"I also use it," Paolo said, "to brush my teeth with."

We set off together on the short stage which would take us that day to León, and to what was considered to be the second great cathedral on the route. Of León it was also boasted that you could visit a different bar every day for a year and still not have visited them all.

Paolo was familiar with every tree and shrub that we passed, the flora of the Spanish Meseta being similar to the landscape in which he had grown up in Portugal. Only after marrying a girl from his village, and coming to realize that they had nothing further to say to each other, had he moved to the capital.

"We got married because I got her pregnant. There was no trouble when it came to that. Naturally I send her money whenever I can."

In Lisbon he had worked, among other things, as a waiter in a bar, and this had been as good as attending a university. Not only had he learned the ways of the world, but he had picked up a smattering of various languages, something which would come in useful if, as he hoped, he succeeded in obtaining a post with an important international company.

"They advertise all over Portugal. They want salesmen, and they say that there's no limit to how much an employee of their company can earn providing that he's willing to work hard."

Paolo rubbed the stubble on his chin. On the other hand, he might not be taken on, or the job might not be as described for he had long since learned that the better something was made to sound, the less likely it was to be true. Or then again the ad might be genuine, and for once in his life he would have a little luck.

The first stretch of the Camino Francés had entailed passing through the mountains of the Basque country. Here the pilgrim, coming up against one obstacle after another, was tested physically. Then came the Meseta, this lonely tableland where, according to the modern-day lore of the Camino, the landscape forced the pilgrim to turn inward and to re-evaluate the life that he or she had so far led. The first phase of the Camino, by this scheme, called for courage, and the second, for forgiveness.

Paolo was dismissive of this way of talking about the Camino.

"Listen. Last year my son became ill and I said that I'd walk the Camino if he got better. Not my son with my wife, you understand, the one that I made later with a woman in Lisbon…"

He wasn't used to a beard, he couldn't stop rubbing his chin.

"Listen, Roberto, I haven't forgotten how you helped me out that time in the snow, but it makes me feel like vomiting when I hear people talking such nonsense."

Being anxious to explore the city, I checked into a hotel in the old quarter. Nothing in my life has given me greater pleasure than exploring a new city, one that can be explored on foot and at random, with no specific itinerary or schedule to meet, and with no need for a map apart from that one which, with every new turning, was taking shape in my head.

Just as I was starting to feel hungry, I found a small corner restaurant promising *comidas caseras*. A couple ran the restaurant on their own, the wife providing the home-cooking while her husband waited on the dozen or so tables, which were spread over three floors. I was first brought an *entremés*, a platter of cold cuts, followed by *albóndigas*, home-made Spanish meatballs. Afterwards I apologized to the *patrón* for having drunk rather more of the bottle of wine than the half bottle to which the menu entitled me.

"It's nothing," he assured me. "Wine isn't measured here by the inch."

He cleared the table, disappeared downstairs, and returned with a homemade flan. Then came the by now familiar question.

"*¿Es usted alemán?*"

Outside the streets were largely deserted, and many of the shops were now shuttered. Having no idea where I was, I looked around until I caught a glimpse of the spires of the cathedral and then made my way in that direction as best I could through the ancient twisting streets.

Who, today, were the true pilgrims? Those carrying credit cards and mobile phones, or those like Paolo who managed to survive on just tomato paste? In the book that Shirley MacLaine wrote after her own pilgrimage, she observed that well-to-do pilgrims walked faster, as they were more goal-oriented, but that they didn't *become* the Camino.

Outside the cathedral I paused to watch a street juggler plying his trade. He too, according to what was scribbled on the scrap of cardboard he had placed on the pavement, considered himself to be a pilgrim.

"Every donation of one euro," it read, "takes me a kilometre closer to Santiago."

Was this the way? Had I encountered at last, here in León, in the shadow of its cathedral, a pure pilgrim? Had he *become* the Camino? Perhaps, but he was certainly no great shakes as a juggler.

Even in the churches and the cathedrals I was now beginning to feel at home. Taking out my notebook, I began circling the nave of the second great cathedral on the Camino. Which were the images housed here? What scenes were portrayed? What stories of the Camino were to be read in the stonework and paintings?

Someone hissed at me. I hadn't even noticed the woman sitting there. Her eyes met mine, and she made a gesture which I failed at first to understand. Had my moving about disturbed her prayers? Had she recognized that I was no true pilgrim, but merely a spectator? A dilettante? A tourist? The woman gestured again, and I then realized what it was. She wanted to draw my attention to the stained glass windows.

◆

The pilgrim was never far from a rendering of one of the wonders associated with the saint to whose tomb his steps were day by day conducting him. Here the pilgrim might peruse the miraculous arrival in Galicia of the marble boat bearing the Apostle's remains, there the miraculous transformation of the wild bulls of Queen Lupa, elsewhere an illustration of the shameful tribute of the Hundred Maidens to which the miraculous appearance of the Apostle, armed, at the battle of Clavijo, would put an end.

Not only the Apostle but the Virgin as well might be portrayed as a pilgrim, *La Virgen Peregrina*. Christ too had on occasion come to the rescue of a pilgrim, thus the image of the *Cristo del Amparo*, whose tiny feet recalled the story of how the Saviour had exchanged his feet for those of a child crippled since birth, thereby making it possible for the child to walk the Camino.

The mythology of Saint James adorned the Camino from beginning to end, and thus even the most solitary pilgrim need never have felt alone. His spirits would at every turn have been lifted, his steps quickened, and his faith strengthened by what he saw about him: for so long as reading remained an accomplishment of the few, seeing would for the most part have been believing.

A mythology is a compendium, an encyclopaedia before the fact, and what it transmits must first of all be relevant. A myth need not reflect a natural or scientific reality so long as it strikes a chord, and conversely, what does reflect "objective" truth may hold no sway if it contradicts what we judge to be true.

A myth situates us in the world. Mythical thinking, it has been suggested, may constitute a specific form of consciousness, one related to the very organizing principles of the human mind. Myths provide a satisfying way of thinking about, and navigating through, a world which we might otherwise experience as intimidating, threatening, overwhelming. Whether or not we navigate the world as pilgrims, myths console us by providing us with a reassurance which the world, as it is, withholds.

Within a mythology each individual myth can be seen both to be supported by, and at the same time to strengthen others which share the same assumptions. Myths, even within the same tradition, need not always agree, and may even provide diverse accounts of the same occurrence without causing the least consternation. In the realm of myth, even contradictory explanations are better than none.

◆

It felt strange to wake up in the morning and not be packing my rucksack. It was still turned inside out to air, as was my sleeping bag. My boots, having been cleaned and re-waterproofed, would also be getting a day off.

I took the stairs down to the lobby of the hotel, avoiding the lift. I wasn't yet ready to re-enter the world of elevators, escalators, and moving walkways. Being in sore need of some new t-shirts, however, I would have to pay a visit later to El Corte Inglés, a department store.

León, with its large Jewish population, had once been renowned for its esoteric studies. It was said that this was where the Kabala had first been concocted, and it was to León, and the house of an ancient Jew, that a French alchemist famously came in the guise of a pilgrim, in search of the key to a certain hermetic text, the meaning of which he had up until then found baffling. The path by means of which so many had walked seeking redemption was by the time of the Renaissance already a path on which others sought enlightenment.

I had my first coffee of the day in a *ciber café*. There was an e-mail from Angelika, saying that her ankle was no better but she would nevertheless be arriving in the city by midday and would meet me at the cathedral.

"Well, Bob," she wrote, "this is the Camino. Lots of pain and irritations. Probably you are laughing at me when you read this. Also I need very much indeed to wash my clothings."

Marisol had written me as well. She and Martín were still walking but doing so slowly, a little each day, and they had so far made it across the Meseta only as far as Sahagún, where they had enjoyed a very good dinner the previous evening. That was nothing, however, compared to the feast that Martín was already planning for them to mark the occasion of their eventually reaching Santiago. She closed with more or less the same words of encouragement which I had noticed spray-painted here and there on pavements and bridge abutments.

"*¡Anímate, peregrino! Buen Camino.*"

To which the correct response, pilgrim to pilgrim, was: "*Igualmente.*"

Although she appeared just at the time she had indicated, and although she managed what was for this sometimes dour young woman a fulsome smile, it was at once clear that Angelika had not exaggerated her plight.

She had been to see a *fisioterapeuta* the evening before, having found his card pinned to the wall of the refuge where she was staying. After examining her ankle, he told her that the only way he could treat the tendon would be if she agreed to keep off her feet for a few days.

"I said to him that I would like to think about it, and he then became very angry. I could think about it if I liked, he shouted very loudly, but in the meantime I owed him ten euros!"

We put all our dirty clothes into a bundle, and dropped it off at a laundry for washing. I then took her to the restaurant which I had discovered the day before, where the patrón, after shaking my hand, recommended that we try the stuffed peppers.

"My wife can stuff anything," he boasted, "even tomatoes. And I didn't even find out about that until after I married her."

The meal was as tasty as on the day before, and eating was something that Angelika enjoyed and to which she gave her full concentration. Only when the last of the empty plates had been removed and we were sitting over coffee did she comment on the window beside us, which, with its small panes, she thought more typical of Switzerland than of Spain.

"Who will I talk to if I stop to rest?" she then blurted. "I will no longer know anyone. What will I be doing with myself all day long?"

"Just what you're supposed to be doing. Resting. Maybe you could read a book."

"Which book? How will I be able to? Everyone else will be going their separate ways."

I would miss her as well. I watched as she stirred a sugar cube into her *café solo*. I could perhaps do without her sour face first thing in the mornings, but what a pleasure to see her in the evening after her shower and her day's walking, sitting out in the sun braiding her hair.

The afternoon was warm, and neither of us had any wish to be indoors. We found our way to a small park and stretched out on the grass. Looming over us was the Basilica of San Isidoro, which contained not only the relics of the great scholar but also, in its Royal Pantheon, the remains of twenty-three kings and queens, twelve princes, and nine counts.

"Everything here is so old," Angelika sighed. "Everything happened such a long time ago. I am sometimes getting tired of hearing about it."

"And everything in Switzerland is new, and efficient, and precise?"

"I am sometimes getting fed up with Switzerland as well."

She took out her mobile and checked to see if any calls had come through. She spoke nearly every day to her mother, whom she had told me was also her best friend. Her father, on the other hand, had left when she was still a child, and it was of him that she now began to speak.

"He had another woman. I was too young even to know what that meant. It was a big mystery to me why he had suddenly disappeared."

From the age of six she had no contact with her father for over ten years, and when they did eventually meet again it was by accident. She was going home from school, walking down a busy street with a classmate.

"I saw him coming towards us on the pavement and I was so happy. Naturally I ran to greet him, and I am still today seeing his face. He thought that I was some crazy person."

For ten years he had never once written to her, and now he no longer even recognized her. She would have changed much more than he had in ten years, she now realized, but that had not occurred to her at the time.

"Angelika?" he echoed, flustered. "You must pardon my not knowing you. My life has at times been very difficult."

She could still remember how she had stood there frozen in the street, not knowing what to do. Ought she to run away from him? Embrace him? Offer him her hand? Her father, equally ill at ease, finally pointed towards the entrance of a shop.

"Come, Angelika. Let me buy you something."

I couldn't be sure how old I was at the time, I couldn't even say for certain that mine was a true story, as most of the details had long since faded. What mattered, in any case, was less the truth of the story than its accuracy, its incorporation of all of the other stories of the times that my own father had, in my opinion, let me down.

I had pestered him for weeks about a film that I wanted to see, and at last he agreed to take me. I looked forward to it for days beforehand, taking care not to misbehave in any way that would give him an excuse for changing his mind. At last the day came and I climbed into the car, at which point he told me that I was old enough to go by myself.

Angelika was by this time sitting up, with her tanned legs clutched tightly to her chest, regarding me with rapt attention.

"My heart was in my mouth. He dropped me off at the theatre, promising to pick me up when the film was over. It was an evening showing, and I seemed to be the only child who had been left there alone."

At last the lights were dimmed. I sat slumped down in my seat, scarcely aware of what was being projected onto the screen. Such was my dread of the moment when the performance would end, and the lights would come up, and I would once more be exposed to scrutiny.

"I didn't wait. As soon as the credits began to roll, I forced my way to the aisle and raced out through the lobby to the street, expecting my father's car to be waiting beside the curb."

The car was nowhere to be seen, and people were by this time filing out of the theatre. I shrank, feeling utterly humiliated. After a time the employees began leaving as well, and the lights in the lobby were switched off. Then even the lights of the marquee were extinguished. And this was where the memory always ended.

"He must have shown up eventually," I concluded, "and I suppose he must have made some excuse or other."

"Probably," Angelika surmised, "he was all the time with his mistress."

"This was Virginia, not Europe. More likely, he was closing a deal."

"What would it mean, 'closing a deal?'"

"Signing a contract on a house or a piece of property. As likely as not the signing would have taken place on the hood of his car."

My father, in those days, had been in real estate. And before that, after leaving the army, he had been in used cars. We had lived in a series of different apartments and houses, and once, for six months, we lived in a motel in Las Vegas, my father having come up with a system for betting on roulette which he was sure would break the bank.

"Spaniards go to Compostela, Americans to Las Vegas."

Angelika stared at me, uncertain as to whether I had meant this as a joke. Yes, I said, my father too had been a pilgrim, always setting off in some new direction in search of something better. On paper my father, being of Irish descent, could have been called a lapsed Catholic, but that was ancient history: the real religion of my father, for he had indeed had a religion, had been Free Enterprise.

◆

The year was 1434, and the hero this time was Don Suero de Quiñones, a *caballero*, the oldest son of a noble family of León, and a self-proclaimed prisoner of love. As the feast day of the blessed Apostle approached that year, Don Suero, wearing an iron band around his neck as an emblem of his servitude, swore to break three hundred lances in a jousting tournament to take place on the very route of the Camino as it passed from León to Astorga, on the bridge at Hospital de Órbigo.

Permission for the joust having been obtained from the king, Don Suero along with nine companions commenced his defence of the bridge fifteen days before the saint's fiesta. The challenge was to hold out against all comers for thirty days, with the actual day of the saint's festivities being declared a day of truce. A pavilion was erected on the riverbank below, and a kitchen constructed, so that noble spectators might banquet while observing the course of the combat.

Any horseman arriving at the bridge had first to give up his lady's glove or garter as a prize to be fought over. Day after day the jousting continued, and when the time had elapsed it was calculated that sixty eight challengers had been defeated and one hundred and seventy six lances broken, somewhat less than the promised three hundred but still sufficient to release Don Suero from his "captivity." And it only remained then to honour the Apostle with a visit.

Amongst the ex voto offerings already to be found in the cathedral at Compostela were sets of chains left by those warriors released through the intercession of the saint from captivity by the Moors, and so Don Suero's offering, as a token of his own release, was a golden collar. Thus concludes one story, *El Paso Honroso de Don Suero de Quiñones*, but from this story, some have speculated, may have sprung another, that of perhaps the most authentic of Spanish heroes, as recounted by Don Miguel de Cervantes.

◆

I set off from the hotel early and walked out of León by the light of its streetlamps, wanting to be back in the countryside by the time the sun rose. Angelika was no child, and in any case no child of mine. The first responsibility of each pilgrim today was said to be that he or she take full responsibility for his or her self, and to assume too much responsibility for others was as much of an error as to accept too little.

The sun had risen long before I was out of the suburbs, and the first few hours of the day were hard work, as the way was never far from busy roads. The route was neither easy to follow nor easy to walk on account of the constant traffic, with the sole diversion being a modern rendering of the saint on the façade of a church, a *Santiago Peregrino* pointing the way westwards to his city and his shrine.

I dug out a hat with a brim from my rucksack, as the sun was hot. Now and again, where the route of the Camino ran along the verge of the highway, the driver of a vehicle flashing past gave a toot on the horn by way of encouragement, a passing greeting which I never failed to return with a wave of appreciation.

That day the towns offered little more of interest than the highway. By midday the traffic had dropped off and they became ghost towns as the inhabitants settled down to their midday meals. I walked mechanically, paying little attention to anything around me, content to count down the kilometres still to be covered before I reached the next refuge.

The table was set out on the pavement, just in front of someone's door, and thus impossible to miss. Resting on the table was a wicker basket containing fruit, nuts, and small packets of biscuits.

"Pilgrims," a hand-written sign read, "this is for you."

Although I was carrying ample food to see me through the day, this simple act of kindness stopped me in my tracks. I helped myself to a clementine and some peanuts. Before daring to knock, I listened at the door, hoping to hear the sound of voices. Nothing. I was curious as to who lived there, but my gratitude, I judged, would be better expressed by leaving a note than by disturbing anyone's siesta.

It wasn't at all difficult, standing on the famous bridge at Hospital de Órbigo, to recreate the event which had once taken place there. Pairs of horsemen with levelled lances would have charged each other headlong from opposite ends of the bridge, while in the meadow below a scene would be unfolding which combined the formality of a stately banquet with the bustle of a country fair.

There was a choice of refuges in which to stay, one in the town and another in the more secluded setting of a pine forest beside the river. The forest refuge was unlocked, but deserted. Yes, I sometimes felt lonely walking alone in a town or city, past shops and houses with their shutters down, but not here under the pines, surrounded by the birds and butterflies.

It was evening by the time I returned to the town. The air was thick with insects and along the bank of the river there were fishermen trying their luck. Having been directed to a bar offering a *menú de peregrino*, I found two fair-haired and sunburned women of about my own age, already seated in the *comedor*. Switching from German to English, they invited me to join them.

"Do you know any Spanish?" the more serious looking of the two asked. "All that we can recognize on this menu is *espaguetis*."

"And we eat that every night," the other added. "Except also sometimes *macarrones*."

The Spanish dictionary which they origianally carried with them had proved too heavy and so had to be abandoned. Their names were Clara and Petra and they were both friends and colleagues. They challenged me to guess what profession they practiced when back home in Germany. The first thing that came into my head was, "Schoolteachers."

One frowned and one smiled. How had I guessed? Indeed there were more schoolteachers on the Camino than any other profession, Clara informed me while Petra merely laughed. The average pilgrim from Germany moreover, it had been reported in their teaching journal, was between forty-five and fifty years old, and slightly more likely to be male than female.

"And that's the sort of thing they put in your teaching journal?"

"Yes, of course. As well as items of purely pedagogical interest."

I found myself, as the meal progressed, speaking less to Clara and more to Petra. She had a ready laugh, and gave the impression that she was doing the pilgrimage above all in order to enjoy herself. She had not really prepared properly for the Camino, she admitted, and so walked very slowly, stopping to smell the flowers.

"But also because my feet are hurting."

Their spring holiday was nearly over already and there was now no chance of their making it to Santiago on this attempt, which was just what their husbands had predicted. It would have been more sensible to have taken up golf, their husbands thought, than to go traipsing off through Spain with rucksacks on their backs at their age.

"I think," said Petra, with her eyes full of mischief, "that they just like to know where we are."

A fourth pilgrim appeared in the doorway and made a beeline to join us. He was an Austrian and already well acquainted with the two women.

He summoned the waiter and ordered at once, as we were already onto our second course.

"You should have waited for me," he complained to the women. "So now I will punish you by making you jealous."

He produced a mobile phone and was soon speaking to his wife. The conversation was in German and it was, according to Petra, all lies. No sooner had this first call been completed than the man made a second call, this time to his mistress, with whom he was planning to meet up in Santiago.

"The fellow is a swine," Petra whispered, "but we have a plan."

They had been speaking about it that day as they walked. First they would get hold of the Austrian's phone while he in the shower and they would use it to call his wife themselves and suggest that she should come to Santiago as well.

"Don't you think," said Petra, "that he would have a nice surprise?"

COSAS DEL CAMINO

✠

The image that does not embrace male and female
is not a high and true image.

The Zohar

A myth is a linguistic tool, and one of great flexibility. A myth deals in images and symbols, bypassing reasoned argument in order to address what reason has failed to unravel. Myth's first and last resort is metaphor, making us see one thing as another, mixing up the natural and supernatural, men and gods, the dead and the living, operating where meaning otherwise eludes us, holding up for inspection what would otherwise never be seen by the light of day. Myths smuggle in what, in the realm of reason alone, would be confiscated at the border.

The structure of a myth resembles nothing so much as the structure of a dream, and might this resemblance not reflect more than mere coincidence? Might not what today appear to us the most illogical and fantastical of myths have begun life as nothing more or less than the telling of a dream? What more likely source could there be for the fabulous and uncanny creatures which we find populating humankind's earliest fantasies than man's own, nascent, but already pro-active consciousness?

A myth is an aesthetic creation of the human imagination. A myth, whether or not its content first passed to the surface of consciousness via a dream, is something wrought. In the telling and retelling, a multiplicity of hitherto unconscious elements is brought forth and a coherent chain of events fashioned from what was to begin with random and chaotic. The first stage of human understanding was, and is, the telling of a good story.

Is it too facile, or fanciful, to imagine, as some have done, the dreams of individuals being forged, over time, into the myths which are the dreams of the group? A dream, in order to be recalled, needs be meaningful only to the dreamer, whereas a myth requires the waking consent of others as to its probity: a myth need not treat objective reality, reality as it really is, but only an agreed reality, reality as it appears, the lowest common denominator of reality.

The dream of an individual, as it evolved into a myth, would have in the process become the property of all. To listen to a myth, or hear a story has always been a concrete experience. What we hear shapes us. And what has shaped us, we will later cling to and defend, sometimes fighting even to the death to do so.

Humankind has been nothing if not prodigal with its creations, and we cherish nothing so much as what we ourselves have invented. There is but one night sky above, but there are many zodiacs. And the day sky too has for long been the abode of gods, which latterly we have made into God, careful, in our increasingly sophisticated and quasi-rational theology, to situate Him well beyond the range of our telescopes.

◆

Having had the pine forest refuge completely to myself, I was woken up not by the usual whispers and shuffling noises of early-rising pilgrims, but by the singing of forest birds. A mist lay over the river and the pines as I set off, and I was nearly upon a pair of deer before they spied me and fled deeper into the forest. Awake for only an hour and already the day's first surprise.

I had not been long on the road when, passing through a hamlet of no more than half a dozen small farms, I was hailed by someone from her window.

"*Buenos días, peregrino. ¿Te apetece una crepa?*"

The woman met me at her kitchen door with a plate. She rolled up one of the freshly made crepes and sprinkled it with sugar. It was still warm, light, and delicious.

"*¿Alemán?*" she asked.

No, not German, I lived in Scotland, which bordered England. Even before I had finished the first *crepa*, she pressed a second on me. And how, she wanted to know, were these called in Scotland?

"Pancakes."

I noticed the small saucer then with a small label stuck to it: *Donativos*. As the Camino passed right through the yard of her farm, she could spot any approaching pilgrims while still standing over her stove, and so intercept them. This, in Britain, where it was at that time being extolled, would have been called diversification.

She walked with me as far as the next gate.

"You're so slim," she remarked. "It's not healthy. Don't you have a wife?"

"Yes, but not with me."

"How unfortunate. How far do you walk each day?"

"Some days twenty kilometres, some days thirty."

"*¡Vaya! ¡Qué sufrimiento!*"

I reached Astorga, my destination for the day, in good time, and just as a bike race was about to set off from the town's main plaza. By standing on a park bench I was able to see over the heads of the spectators who were already lining the route. A horn was sounded to signal the start of the race, upon which perhaps a hundred riders set off at a most sedate pace, preceded by policemen on motorcycles and followed by team cars with their roof racks full of spare bicycles.

Someone took my arm and a schoolgirl hoisted herself up beside me.

"Is that all?" she asked. "What a disappointment! Is this what they let us out of school for?"

The race would not begin in earnest until the riders were outside the town. Meanwhile the crowd was already dispersing, the traffic cones were being gathered, and the plaza was returning to normal. Some five hours from now the race would conclude in a different town, and we would be able to watch the finish live on television.

The schoolgirl, before heading off, shook my hand.

"*Usted es alemán, ¿verdad?*"

Astorga was the chief town of the Maragataría region. Above the town hall clock an automated Maragato couple in traditional dress struck the hours. There was a cathedral to visit, and the bishop's palace, designed by Gaudí. The town was also partially encircled by a Roman wall.

On my way to the *albergue* I met two Japanese pilgrims pushing mountain bikes, an elderly gentleman with a white beard and a younger man whom I guessed to be his son. The younger pilgrim offered me his hand, the older one bowed.

"How far have you come today?" I asked.

"We come from Japan," the son replied.

"Today, I mean. Where did you start from this morning?"

"Yes, my father is old, but he is very well, thank you."

Later, in the town's *ciber café,* I found an e-mail from Angelika, who was spending a further day resting in León but hoped to be back on the move again soon.

"I am being very good," the message continued. "I am following other people's advice for once. I am even calm, Bob, you will be certainly surprised to hear."

Everything in the bar came to a halt as, on the television, the cyclists in the race were reaching the end of that day's stage. There was great excitement as they jockeyed for position for the final sprint, with even the waiters pausing in their work to watch. It might be only a minor race, but who knew when the next Pedro Delgado or Miguel Indurain might emerge?

One of the riders sat up, raising his arms in triumph.

"Is it over?" Lawrence asked. "Would it be possible, do you suppose, for us to get another drink now?"

We were waiting for the pizzeria to open. Lawrence was determined that we should eat there because a quick perusal of the menu had revealed that it was nearly identical to that outside his favourite pizza restaurant back home in Manchester. He said he had very nearly burst into tears while reading the menu.

The restaurant that evening was packed with pilgrims. Once again, two streams had come together, the route from Granada and Seville having joined the Camino Francés. Amongst the other diners were the two Japanese, whom Lawrence had also encountered that day.

"The old boy was just about bearable, but the young one thought that he could speak English. He speaks about as much English as I speak Japanese."

"And just how much Japanese would that be, I wonder?"

"*Kamikaze* and *sayonara*, just like any other well-bred Englishman."

I returned alone to the refuge, leaving Lawrence to go in search of a few more "quiet drinks." The two German women, Petra and Clara, had only just arrived and were still sitting in the reception room of the refuge catching their breath. Petra got to her feet and we embraced like two old friends.

"How did you manage to take so long?" I asked. "Did you get lost? It was only half a day's walk."

"Didn't I tell you before?" said Petra. "We always stop to smell the flowers, and also the coffee. Five times today we had to stop to smell the coffee. And then, of course, we needed to find places with a toilet."

◆

The Maragatos were the fabled mule drivers of Spain. To a nineteenth century visitor, George Borrow, they were slow and plain of speech, strong but also brutish and heavy, pragmatic in constitution but dangerous and desperate once incensed. What the Maragatos of that time made of the Welshman George Borrow, whose chosen mission was to bring the Bible to Spain, sadly failed to find its way into print.

A more sympathetic observer described the courtship practices of the Maragatería. A suitor, by way of declaring his intentions, was required to lay down a trail of straw from the door of his house to the door of his intended, who, if her own fancy resided elsewhere, simply continued the trail down to the river.

A Maragato woman, once won, according to Richard Ford, was a model of constancy. The Maragato bride, on her wedding day, wore a *manto*, a full length cape, never donning it again afterwards until the day of her husband's death. Also worthy of note were the hearty appetites of the Maragatos. Newlyweds, before rising from their conjugal bed, were expected to consume between them, for their wedding breakfast, a pair of roasted chickens.

Carnival in the Maragatería, which as elsewhere included what would at any other time of the year have been condemned as blasphemy, involved masked revellers "baptizing" all and sundry from sacks full of ashes. A domestic beast which had recently died was then dissected in order that its various parts could be distributed appropriately, with the local gossip, for instance, being presented with the tongue.

Carnival combined licence with custom. A Maragato gentleman wishing to dance with a Maragato lady was obliged first to hook her by the legs with a curved crook. The Maragato children, having gathered ants from the fields, would let them loose on the dance floor so that they might, as the dance progressed, crawl up under the Maragato ladies' skirts.

The new year was marked by the Fiesta del Arado, the Festival of the Plough. Shepherds dressed as women were given the task of ploughing a single furrow around the lands of each Maragato village, up the mountainside and down. An equivalent practice, persisting to this day in the Borders region of Scotland, goes by the name of Riding the Marches.

◆

It was the worst night's sleep that I had so far suffered. The bunk above me had been occupied by an immense pilgrim who not only snored without cease the whole night through, but so strained the springs of his bed that they had sagged to within a few inches of my chest. What price now the peace and the silence of the *albergue* in the pine forest?

In the morning the sky was clear, promising a fine day. There was a motorway to be crossed, but the route then led out into the countryside, towards a distant range of mountains. Twice that morning, after stops for coffee, I found myself overtaking Giovanni and Sofia.

"*¡Hola, Roberto!* Are you well today?"

"Very well, thank you. Despite having slept under a bear last night."

"*Cosas del Camino, Roberto, cosas del Camino.*"

The second time I came upon them they were seated beside a fountain enjoying a small picnic. Spread out on a napkin were slices of fruitcake, some almonds, and Italian figs which had been steeped in a sweet liqueur. They had carried all of these things with them from home, they explained, in order to celebrate their wedding anniversary.

"Always we celebrate in the *campagna*," Giovanni said. "We have a house there, and all of our children come, and nowadays they bring their own children."

They insisted that I join them in their celebration. Although they walked slowly, they never appeared to be tired, and when resting, even on the ground, they always sat just as they walked, with their backs straight, never slouching. Nor could I remember, even on the wettest of days, having ever seen them muddy.

I asked if, after their first Camino, they had found it hard going back home afterwards. Not so hard, Giovanni said, as he had a job waiting for him, and Sofia had been showing the first signs of being pregnant. The job had been at the university at which he had at the time only recently completed his studies, and it was from this very same university, just weeks before setting off on this second pilgrimage, that he had retired.

I congratulated him on a life so orderly and dignified.

"Some would say 'ordinary,'" said Giovanni.

A few years ago he had planted some vines, and these would soon be reaching maturity. He would soon be finding out whether or not he had a "green thumb." Sofia, meanwhile, had their grandchildren to keep her busy, and she had also joined a club for reading novels.

"So now you know, Roberto, what it's like to grow old."

The destination that day was the village of Rabanal del Camino. The Refugio Gaucelmo, which was operated by the Confraternity of Saint James back in London, had not yet opened, but already, outside the door, a queue of rucksacks and boots had formed.

Not long after my own arrival, a taxi pulled into the courtyard to disgorge a large Scotsman wearing a kilt. His name was Alistair and he was there to take over as *hospitalero*, but as he could raise no one inside the refuge there was nothing for it but for us to go in search of a beer.

He explained, over our first drink, just how it worked. All of the *hospitaleros* at Gaucelmo were volunteers, they served for two weeks at a stretch, and they paid their own air fares. At that time of the year, when the number of pilgrims was still low, they worked in pairs, usually a man and a woman. Alistair's partner for the next fortnight, whom he had yet to meet, was to be a Frenchwoman.

In neither of the two village bars were we allowed to pay for our own drinks. Relations with the villagers were generally good, and Alistair's kilt was a real ice breaker. Only once had he experienced any difficulty, and that was with the first *hospitalera* with whom he had been paired.

"She was English, and she was a real stickler for the rules. There was a football match on television one night and some of the pilgrims were watching it in the bar. When it was nearly curfew time I went to fetch them, and what do you suppose she did?"

He paused to shake hands with the proprietor of the bar, who had just returned from a shopping trip to Astorga. Two more *cañas* were then placed in front of us at the invitation of the house.

"Where was I? On yes, I was telling you about how that silly woman locked us all out that night. We had a devil of a time, but we finally got in through a window. Did I mention that she was English?"

They were not exactly speedy, but they did manage to arrive in time to get the last two beds in the refuge before the "*Completo*" sign was hung out. We laughed out loud as soon as we saw each other, embraced, and then laughed again at this ridiculous behaviour.

"You'll love it here," I informed Petra. "There's a machine that will spin your clothes after you've washed them."

"The English too are practical," Clara pronounced. "Very similar to the Germans."

Later, when their clothes were on the line, we sat in the garden waiting to be summoned to the chapel for a vespers service. Petra's plan, when her career in teaching was over, was to take up sculpture. Art had been her favourite subject in school, but she had allowed herself to be swayed by the argument that becoming a teacher would be more sensible.

"Clara can tell you. I have usually been sensible, but not always."

"And it was her," Clara concurred, "who said that we should do this Camino."

Petra thought that she might have an aptitude for art, but how could she be sure? She had taken courses over the years, and her work, although that of a mere beginner, was said to show promise. On the other hand, perhaps all the students had been told that so as not to discourage them.

The chapel bell started chiming. There were only a few pews, but people squeezed over to make room for us. The building was Romanesque, and the mass, which was celebrated by two monks, was in Gregorian chant.

Clara claimed afterwards not to be feeling well. All that she had any appetite for was her bed and a good night's sleep, and certainly not for any more Spanish food. Tomorrow they would be turning around and returning to Astorga to begin the long journey back to Germany.

"So you must behave yourselves," Clara told us outside the chapel. "And you must not forget the curfew."

"Yes, mother," said Petra.

Only when we had sat down at the small table for two and ordered our meal did it suddenly dawn on us that we really knew little about each other, and that the circumstances under which we were sitting there were really quite extraordinary and probably unlikely to be repeated in either of our lives. Suddenly it felt as though we were out on a date, with all the awkwardness which, even at our age, this entailed.

Various pilgrims that one or the other of us knew only casually came and went with nods of acknowledgment. In two days' time, Petra reflected, she would be back in Germany, back to her husband and her job.

"And I will not even have visited Santiago, isn't that sad?"

"Not necessarily. Santiago will remain for the next time."

"But I never finish things. Always I become frightened and unsure and start looking back over my shoulder."

"At Clara?"

"Yes, I think so. Sometimes I say to myself how lucky we are to have been friends for so long, and sometimes I say just the opposite."

The kitchen was busy, and we had a long wait for our meal. Petra was toying with some bread, moulding it with her fingers, whereas I, recalling the story that Alistair had told me about the strict *hospitalera*, was wondering about which window we might have to crawl back in through.

I told Petra then that of all the people I had met so far on the Camino, she was the one who seemed to be enjoying it the most. The seriousness left her face and some of the joy which I had noted earlier returned.

"Some days we did only five miles. One of the *hospitaleros* said that we were just tourists and refused to let us stay in his *albergue*."

"Better a happy tourist, I suppose, than a sour pilgrim."

"But we were both very cross that night, do you know why? Not because the hotel was too expensive, but because we were ashamed of how time was slipping through our fingers."

◆

Myths and rituals, it has often been remarked, go hand in hand. What the myth explains, the rite acts out, and vice versa. The bulk of human knowledge is received knowledge, and the favoured vehicles for the transmission of that knowledge have ever been just what we may be tempted to dismiss as mere baseless fantasy and mindless rites.

A society weaves webs of significance, in the famous phrase of Clifford Geertz, in which the individual members of that society are suspended. We do not, upon entering the world, begin from scratch. Not through our own devices alone do we discover what the wider world holds, what dangers it presents and what good it contains, or what hidden powers order and maintain it. Not by instinct alone do we set our course, human instinct having long since been corralled by legislation.

Myth, having initially been charged with providing the explanation, the rationale behind the impositions laid by the social order upon its members, had next to address the vexatious issue of what occurs when those impositions bind. When, after all, has the course of human life ever run smooth? When has custom, presented as a necessary template for human behaviour, not also constrained, and chaffed?

Myth, by and large, conserves and supports the status quo. A myth may nevertheless hold suspended in its narration not only what is considered to be certain and correct and beyond redress, but also the consequences that follow when such an understanding, such a structuring of the world is challenged or transgressed. The outcome is sometimes comic, sometimes tragic: a good myth, like all good fiction, looks at both sides of the human predicament, and, like the best science, it explains without explaining away.

◆

Albert the Belgian was the first to leave the dormitory that morning, and once he was on his way I dragged my own belongings out into the corridor. Alistair, the *hospitalero*, was already in the kitchen slicing bread for the breakfast which Gaucelmo was noted for offering its guests. I lent a hand, drank a coffee, and then, with my rucksack packed and waiting, I slipped back into the dormitory.

Petra was awake. She had a lower bunk, Clara the bunk above. As I crouched beside her, Petra reached out and found my face, running her hand over it in the dark, memorizing my face as a blind person might have done.

The music for a Gay Gordon, a Scottish country dance, began to blare through the refuge, and it was once more time to let go and be on my way. There were mutters of discontent behind me in the dormitory as the lights were switched on.

Three more days of walking would bring us into Galicia, which the mythology of the Apostle James had first placed on the map of Europe and more recently on that of the world. The path climbed up from the village of Rabanal, and I was soon looking out across a wide panorama of peaks and valleys. Villages nestled here and there in the laps of the valleys and higher up the slopes, amongst the rocks, were the pens and shelters of shepherds.

I passed Foncebadón without encountering any of the packs of wild dogs that were rumoured to roam its ruins. At the Cruz de Ferro, where an iron cross rose out of a immense cairn, I found a party of Brazilian tourists. Having just descended from their bus, they lacked only a pilgrim or two to pose before the cross.

Pilgrims were encouraged to bring a pebble with them from their homelands to lay on the cairn, but I had not. Scotland's stones for the Scots! Nor had I brought a list of my sins to affix to the cross, although not, of course, for want of any.

The curious village of El Acebo consisted of a single narrow street. The houses which lined the way on either side, with their low balconies, seemed to be leaning forward, thus confronting the pilgrim with either a gauntlet to be run or a guard of honour, depending on his mood.

If El Acebo appeared to be folded in upon itself, the small resort town of Molinaseca gave precisely the opposite impression. The terraces of its bars and hotels looked out over a river, a swimming pool fed by the river, and the bridge over which newly arrived pilgrims entered the town.

Situated on a hill above the town was the church and its churchyard, and it was there that I went to sit that afternoon to make my notes for the day. To fall behind in my notes for even a single day would mean losing track of the thread that I was convinced must be running through all that I was experiencing. Never mind if I was deceiving myself along the way, for I was well aware that there was probably no end to the various manners of self-trickery of which we were at once the victims and the perpetrators. Nevertheless, with careful notes to hand, I could always go back and revise, refine, straighten out my crooked thinking. What a disaster this whole trip would have been, on the other hand, if I reached Compostela in the best physical condition of my life but without having got to the bottom of anything.

Suddenly my attention was drawn to the far side of the river where a familiar figure was just at that moment making his approach to the bridge. Rushing down from the church, I reached the bridge just in time to intercept Park before he disappeared into the town.

"*¡Hermano!*"

Any number of misadventures had befallen him since we had last met. Not understanding what people were saying to him, he had mistaken the times of buses, and had twice left his stick behind in hotel rooms, but his stay in the monastery of Silos had nevertheless been one of the greatest experiences of his life.

"There are places in the world, brother, where you know for certain that God is present. The proof of this is in that certainty."

There was no point in attacking such a circular argument, at no point was it left undefended. In order to keep to his itinerary, Park then added by way of a confession, he had been forced to skip several long stages on the Meseta, for which he hoped that God would forgive him. He hoped, though, that I wouldn't mention this to Angelika.

"So you're more afraid of Angelika than you are of the deity?"

"The deity, brother, has infinite patience."

DRIVING OUT DEMONS

✠

*At first there is wandering, and wearisome roaming,
and fearful travelling through darkness...*

Plutarch

It is to be doubted whether any culture, any religion, or any state has yet come into being without an attendant mythology to explain its existence. Myths of origin have been, throughout history, both ubiquitous and protean, difficult either to ignore or to refute. A myth of miraculous beginnings is typically multi-faceted, able to empower, motivate, heal, and console. And such narrations persist by evolving, with many a discredited myth simply turning up again later in a new guise.

Each retelling of a myth presents the opportunity for a miss-telling. The remaking of a myth for a new audience is the very process of its evolution, and the result ought not to be judged on the basis of faithfulness to the original, but only as to its continued relevance.

Each new version of a myth adds to its richness. In the realm of myth there is little new under the sun, and the majority that we now possess have their roots in a distant past, in psyches only distantly related to our own.

Unlike the artworks which they may have inspired, myths cannot be looted. A myth is as much a process as a thing. A myth, illuminating with its small light what in its own time cried out for explanation, also serves as a stimulus for other versions and explanations. The model for the transmission of myth is not that of theft or of expropriation, but of one candle being lit from another.

The world as it appears in myths, a world partly observed and partly imagined, is a world that we all still live in some of the time. A perceptive observer of myth has suggested, given its prevalence and its persistence, that the question which ought to be asked of myth is not *what* it is, but *when*.

A myth is likely to be encountered when the facts of a matter are various and complex, and would otherwise elude easy understanding. A myth is to be suspected when critical discernment is short-circuited by wishful thinking, or when what is known to be the case by the best informed few is set aside for the sake of what pleases the majority. There are also times, still, when a myth may be the best available answer.

Myths may at times, and particularly when they are the myths of others, merely provoke mirth, and thus the following entry in the *Devil's Dictionary* of Ambrose Bierce:

> Mythology is the body of a primitive people's beliefs
> concerning its origin, early history, heroes, deities and so forth,
> as distinguished from the true accounts which it invents later.

There may come a time when even our own myths are powerless to move us other than to laughter, but that time, for better or worse, is not yet. The recurring history of man is that whatever we have found or invented that is useful has also proved pernicious, and our most cherished myths have also served as rallying calls, summoning us to do battle on their behalf against those whose inventions are other than our own.

◆

The wood of the sanctuary door of the Virgen de las Angustias, *La Preciosa*, was thought to have miraculous properties. Galician reapers passing through Molinaseca on their way to assist with the harvest in Castilla y León paused at the sanctuary to try their blades, believing that this would preserve the sharpness of their tools for the duration of the harvest. They would pause again at the high point of Cruz de Ferro (which may once upon a time have been a shrine to Mercury, the Roman god of travellers) to drop a stone on the cairn as a warrant for their safe return.

West from Molinaseca was the town of Ponferrada, *Pons ferrata*, named for the iron bridge erected there in the eleventh century by order of the bishop of Astorga, for the convenience of pilgrims. Having arrived in the town early on a Sunday morning, I found nothing open and no one about except a man walking with a newspaper under his arm. As we were heading in the same direction, we soon fell into step, and into conversation.

His name was Carlos, and he lived along the Camino. He made television documentary films, and was thinking of making a film about the Camino and the pilgrims who, in the course of a year, passed through Ponferrada.

"Who are they? Where have they come from? What are they looking for?"

"You'll get as many answers," I predicted, "as there are pilgrims."

"That's just what I'm hoping for. Nothing would be more tedious than the same answer from everyone."

He knew of a bakery nearby that would be open. The baker knew him, and at once put a table and two chairs out onto the pavement so that we could enjoy our coffee and croissants sitting in the sun. One reason for foreigners coming to Spain to walk the Camino, I suggested, might be because they found the Spaniards so accommodating.

"Today, yes," Carlos replied, "but don't forget that it took a civil war before we were able to get along. Visitors can now reap the benefits."

He had never walked the Camino himself, and could not imagine ever doing so. The curiosity aroused by the sight of so many strangers passing through the city, all year long and sometimes in atrocious weather, would soon enough be satisfied once he began filming.

"Also," he added, "memories are long, and some things will never be forgiven. My poor grandfather will be squirming in his grave at the thought of my filming pilgrims."

"But today there are pilgrims of the left as well as the right."

"So I believe. The Church, these days, has a lot to swallow. The dead, however, are fixed in their ways, and any film about pilgrims is certain to create more pilgrims."

The small market town of Cacabelos had been sealed off to all traffic by the Guardia Civil, this being the day of its annual *feria*. The streets were lined with *puestos* from which were being sold all manner of goods from farming implements and culinary delicacies of the Bierzo region, to ominous looking corsets and incredibly capacious brassieres. At the latter stall I met up with two Danish pilgrims, a mother and daughter, who since joining the route a few days earlier had kept completely to themselves.

"Are you just looking," I asked, "or planning to buy?"

"Just wondering," the daughter replied, "whether those bras are to wear or for carrying melons home from the fields."

In the central plaza an octopus feast was already in progress, and we decided to share a *ración* between us. For the preparation of the dish called *pulpo a la feria*, the creatures were first boiled whole in cauldrons, then fished out with a small grappling hook, snipped into bite-size pieces with a scissors, heaped onto wooden platters, and finished off with olive oil, salt, and a sprinkling of paprika.

We found places at a long trestle table, beneath a colourful awning, and were supplied with a loaf of bread, a bottle of red wine, and toothpicks with which to spear the *pulpo*. Flamenco music was blaring from a nearby shop, and one of the local beauties, egged on by her friends, got up to give her version of a flamenco dance.

Christina, the younger of the two Danes, explained, as we were eating, that they were doing the Camino because her mother had recently become a widow. The daughter's English, like her Spanish, was faultless. The mother spoke only Danish and so had to communicate employing a curious sort of sign language, one which included of pointing out certain objects and grimacing disapprovingly.

"Mother has never eaten octopus before," Christina apologized.

The *feria* was an occasion not just for celebration, but also for promotion. There were stands displaying the wines of the Bierzo region, and tables were piled high with the breads of the Bierzo region. Poles were hung with strings of smoked chorizo, and racks were lined with the distinctive pottery of the Bierzo. As we walked on through the town, laden with our rucksacks, we felt as if we belonged there, forming part of the spectacle that day, and representing in our persons and by our passage the centuries old flow of pilgrims through the Bierzo.

Christina, as we were leaving the town, remembered a joke.

"They tell it about the Galicians. It might even be true. Apparently, the translation of *pulpo a la feria* in their English language tourist guides is "Octopus to the fair.""

Villafranca del Bierzo was only one of several Villafrancas on the route, towns populated in medieval times by French pilgrims who had elected not to return to France. At the Ave Fenix, a refuge still in the process of being rebuilt after being previously burned to the ground, I was led up to the dormitory reserved for "*Mayores*," pilgrims of a certain age.

I had washed out some clothes and was hanging them out on the balcony when Park turned up clutching a large cake, a *tarta de manzana* which he had purchased at the *feria* in Cacabelos and which he intended to share that evening with the other pilgrims. Without even bothering to unpack he dragged me back out of the refuge wanting me to help him find the ancient *Puerta del Perdón*.

We located the church and tried the Door of Pardon, but it was locked. Having come this far, any pilgrim who was too ill to proceed further could, in the past, have claimed, simply by passing through this door, the absolution otherwise granted only to those who continued on to the altar of the cathedral in Santiago. God, according to Park, asked no more of us than the maximum of which we were capable.

Tomorrow we would be entering Galicia, not just the resting place of the Apostle but also a region of Spain long associated with witches and witchcraft. And might this not be the reason for the sheaves of what appeared to be a wild herb that people had affixed to the balconies of their houses, just above the front doors? Perhaps these bundles had been blessed by the priest on Palm Sunday. Wasn't it said that God worked in mysterious ways?

Park too had come across the Japanese pilgrims on their bicycles. He had found them sitting beside the road bathing their feet in an irrigation ditch, and had joined them. The elderly father, as it turned out, was a noted calligrapher in Japan, and the son was a designer of computer games.

"It was strange to be talking to such people here in Spain, *hermano*. I asked them why they were making the Camino, and they couldn't even tell me."

"Maybe they were just out riding their bicycles and they made a wrong turn."

"Or maybe they made the correct turn," said Park.

We had been hoping to witnessing a *queimada* ceremony that evening in the *albergue*. This rite, the chief purpose of which was to drive off harmful spirits, required a punch made from *orujo*, a spirit of another sort, of Galician provenance, which was flamed before being poured out. This punch, with its accompanying liturgy of spells, was intended to dispel all malicious forces and so would lift the hearts of the participating pilgrims on the eve of what would be their most difficult day yet on the Camino.

The girl who had been left in charge of the refuge had some bad news.

"Unfortunately Jesús won't be here tonight."

Jesús was Jesús Jato, the proprietor of the Ave Fenix, and he was away at a meeting. The best that could be done in his absence was to provide us with a translation of the incantation into English. A single day of climbing and we would enter the lands of Galicia, with the danger coming only if we began to tire. The spirits were like wolves, the girl warned, and only attacked what they knew to be weak.

White owls and toads, crows and salamanders, the howl of a dog, the scent of the dead, the screech of a cat in heat were the signs and familiars of Satan. Such were the dark spirits against which were called forth the guardian powers of the forces of air, earth, sea, and protecting fire.

Some believed in this and some didn't. The flame of the *queimada*, the girl explained, was meant to put fire into our bellies so that nothing thereafter would frighten us, and not even the mountains would be able to tire us. That was what those who believed in such things thought.

"As for me," the girl added, "if I were going to O Cebreiro, I'd go by car."

◆

One of the most cherished miracles associated with the route of the Camino took place in the church of Santa María la Real, amidst the pallozas, the straw-thatched huts which made up the village of O Cebreiro. The saying of mass in that church had become the responsibility of a lone monk who had come to harbour doubts as to whether the Host contained what it was said to contain. The sacrament which he celebrated each morning in the almost empty church had become for him just one more daily chore.

The miracle occurred one cold winter's morning. A blizzard had struck during the night and left the village buried under a blanket of snow, but when the monk entered the church he found a pilgrim already waiting there, soaking wet and stiff with cold.

"What does this fool expect of me?" the monk asked himself. "Why has he risked his life in such a terrible storm?"

The monk made his usual preparations for celebrating the Eucharist, feeling nothing but pity for the poor soul shivering before him. Did that poor pilgrim truly believe that a few phrases which through countless repetitions the monk knew by heart would be sufficient to bring about the transmutation of a crust of bread and a few swallows of wine into the flesh and the blood of the Son of God?

The monk proceeded as he had long been accustomed to, closing his eyes as he had been taught at the moment of consecration, when his actions were expected to produce that miracle in which all pretended to believe but none had ever yet witnessed. On this occasion, however, feeling an unexpected warmth between his hands, the monk opened his eyes and to his astonishment perceived that that which he purported to perform had actually come to pass, the bread had indeed become flesh and the chalice which had held wine now contained blood.

Does the miracle at O Cebreiro not imply that the simple faith of a pilgrim is a more potent force than either the authority of a church or the rituals of its priests, and is this not just how we would *wish* the world to be? The sacred substances have been preserved in precious vials, gifts of the Catholic Kings, Ferdinand and Isabel. And there was, it came to be claimed, a third witness, in addition to the monk and the pilgrim, to that miraculous proof: a statue of the Virgin which stood beside the altar and at the moment of the miracle bowed its head.

◆

Park, despite having set his alarm and risen early, was not ready to set off. The contents of his rucksack were strewn the length of the balcony, and he still had clothes on the drying racks. Unwilling to delay my own start on what was going to be a long day, I hoisted my rucksack and slipped past him.

"Take care not to get lost," I warned him, "or too exhausted. Remember what that girl said last night about demons."

"Did she say that they looked like wolves? In Korea they look like Chinamen."

Having a choice of three routes that day, I chose the path which rose at once towards the hamlet of Pradela. Walking alone, surrounded by fields and orchards, I felt more than equal to the challenge which the day's climb would present, but ever less certain as to what my own pilgrimage was likely to achieve. Ought I to have had a better plan, a clearer purpose in mind before setting out on the Camino, or might it have been more to my advantage to have had no plan at all?

Beyond Pradela the path descended, joining up with the valley route, and this was where I caught up with Paolo. He too, was beginning to have doubts, especially as the garments which he had set out in from Lisbon were now ripped and torn and left him looking like a beggar.

"But you've come so far, Paolo, and now you're nearly there."

"It's different for you, Roberto. If something wears out, you can replace it and still be able to afford to eat afterwards."

In Paolo's mind this was associated with the fact of my speaking English. English was the language of computers, and thus anyone who spoke English, regardless of their nationality, already had a leg up on anyone who didn't.

"But didn't you tell me that you learned English working in a bar?"

"Yes, but not the right English."

Having reached a cluster of houses, we hoped that we might find a shop in which to buy groceries. The village had no shop of any sort, an old woman in a blue-checked apron told us, not since the people who had last run a shop there had died.

"But wait here a moment," she told us. "Pilgrims can't walk on empty stomachs."

She disappeared into one of the houses, reappearing shortly with half a loaf of bread and some tomatoes, for which she refused to accept any payment. We should go to the last house in the village, she then advised us, knock on the door, and ask for Pili. Pili was her daughter-in-law and she grew onions.

"You shouldn't have tried to pay her," Paolo rebuked me afterwards. "That's what I mean about speaking English. English is the language of business."

"And yet you claim that it embarrasses you to look like a beggar?"

"In English there is only one word for beggar. In Portuguese there are more than a dozen, so don't talk to me about beggars."

Never was nature more enthroned in loneliness, Richard Ford wrote, than in the hills beyond Villafranca. No longer was this entirely true, however, as a motorway now crossed over the valley, entering Galicia by means of a metal and concrete viaduct. As for the spirits, the demons of which we had been warned were no longer lurking in the landscape. Any demons spotted here would be those which we had carried from home.

The route returned to being a mere path and once more began to climb steeply through a forest of chestnut trees, before debouching into the more open country beyond. I was by now alone again, and a steady rain had begun to fall. The track was scarcely visible through my steamed up glasses, nor could I any longer make out the farms nestled in the valley below, but according to my guidebook this was it, the watershed, the homestretch. I had somewhere not too far back entered Galicia.

The trail ended abruptly at a guard rail. Beyond was a tarmac road, and the silence was broken by the sound of a tourist bus struggling up the final incline to the car park at O Cebreiro. Only a few of its ancient *pallozas* remained, the simple huts with their sloped floors in which both the villagers and their livestock had once slept, the villagers at the top of the slope and the animals, along with their effluent, at the bottom.

The refuge was expected to be crowded that night, and we were assigned to the bunks by number. Thus I found myself placed next to a grey-haired woman already stretched out, exhausted, on her mattress.

"We're practically compatriots," I greeted her, indicating the maple leaf that she wore sewn to her rucksack. "I'm one-third Canadian myself."

"One-third? How come? Did you have three parents?"

"No, just three different nationalities."

She was Patricia, from Toronto. This was only her fourth day on the Camino, and by the time I returned from the showers she was sound asleep. I might have had a nap myself had Park not suddenly appeared in the dormitory, soaking wet and distraught.

"You've got to help me, brother. It's a disaster. I left my *credencial* behind in Villafranca."

Not only was the *credencial* a pilgrim's validation, proving that the journey to Compostela had been made in an approved fashion, but it was also, with its many and varied *sellos*, the most cherished souvenir.

The *hospitalera* said that this happened all the time. All sorts of things got left behind, but fortunately there was a daily courier service running between the refuges. She had only to telephone the Ave Fenix, and Park and his precious document would be reunited on the following day.

"Last year," the *hospitalera* added, "someone left behind a wooden leg, and so far no one has reclaimed it. Makes you think, doesn't it?"

It wasn't until after the last of the tourist buses had pulled out that we were able to secure a large enough table in one of the village's small restaurants. Only Paolo, whose plan was to sleep in a barn somewhere along the way, and Angelika, who was at least two days behind, had failed to make it up the mountain. Filling their places within our patched up family were the Canadian Patricia and the two Danes.

People had begun to speak of "real life" again. Suddenly it was becoming impossible not to look ahead to when this would all end. Patricia said that the Camino seemed like a dream in that, however exhausting the day's walk might be, your powers of recovery soon kicked in, and the fatigue was forgotten by the evening.

"And then you wake up the next morning, and you don't even have a hangover."

"As for me," Lawrence offered, "I've always found real life to be greatly over-rated."

"And just who is to say what real life is and what it isn't," Christina contributed, "and on what authority?"

Patricia was a professor of medieval literature. This I learned when we had returned to the dormitory and were lying side by side in our sleeping bags. She was married to a poet and had just been in Paris supervising the birth of her first grandchild.

"So tell me about your three nationalities," she said, "so that I'll know who's sleeping beside me."

There wasn't that much to explain. She had been a student herself during the Vietnam war years and had taken part in demonstrations, so she understood the choice that many of us had faced. It had taken me a bit of time to make the decision, but the rest had been easy. I only had to get into my car and drive north.

The overhead lights had been put out in the dorm, but a few people were still moving about or reading by torchlight. Canada had been a haven, but I had never felt at home there. Probably it hadn't helped that in the ten years that I lived there I had had at least a dozen different addresses.

"What is a Canadian, after all?" said Patricia. "Someone who's proud of not being an American."

We could hear the rain outside being blown against the windows. Somewhere, a few bunks away, the first snoring had commenced. Patricia laughed then, softly, and said that this was certainly a strange end to the day.

"You mean that this is a strange situation in which to be having this sort of conversation?"

"This is a strange situation in which to be having any sort of conversation, I mean, with a man who isn't my husband."

TENDING THE SOUL

✝

We must tell ourselves who we want to be
and then act accordingly.

Epictetus

It would be difficult indeed to describe a human being without a description of what we mean when we speak of a human soul. What has never been seen or measured has nevertheless always been sensed, and named, and what exists in our vocabularies exits in our lives.

We have every reason to believe that the human psyche is unique. Somehow, in the history of humanity, consciousness became self-consciousness. Beginnings are elusive, but perhaps it began with the consciousness of certain of our own feelings, and perhaps this self-awareness surfaced under the light not of the sun, but that of the moon.

Animals also appear to dream, but the immense transformation from mere animal to human being required something more: a more precise language into which to translate the largely symbolic narratives presented by dreams. Humanity and human history, the only history of which we know, may well have commenced with a recitation, an account of a dream which, if it was not itself yet a myth, may well have inspired one.

The soul, like the psyche, is a construct. The facts of the soul are psychological, not physical, and the most basic fact of the soul is, in all probability, the fact of our initial and prolonged helplessness before the world. The most likely "site" of the soul, conceptually, is just at the confluence of the perceptions and the emotions, precisely the conceptual point of our being from which dreams are generated.

The most memorable of the dreams of nascent humankind were no doubt nightmares, and this was not without consequences. What we sense as a soul may be just the memory of how we begin our lives, of our weakness and of our fragility. What human being is not first a helpless infant, unable either to feed or to defend itself, an utterly inadequate creature unable to survive in the world by its own powers alone?

What the soul "knows" and can never for long forget is the *precariousness* of life. We are, so far as we are aware, the only of earth's creatures to have become conscious of its own situation, including the fact of its own inevitable death, and we are as a consequence the most cautious, the most fearful of the creatures which walk the earth, as well as the most ingenious.

◆

Sleeping in a common dormitory with dozens of other pilgrims, some of whom were known to me and some of whom were strangers, had somewhere along the line ceased to be a hardship; it was an essential element of the pilgrimage, necessary if the pilgrimage was to be experienced as an undertaking shared amongst us all. To awaken during the night and to be aware of the breathing of those about me had become as familiar as the rucksacks and the staffs lined up against the wall, the socks draped over the radiators, the wet boots stuffed with crumpled newspapers in the hope that they would be dry by the morning.

The lessons of the Camino taught themselves. That morning in O Cebreiro, when I stepped from the *albergue*, I found the village shrouded in mist. It was only just possible to make out, as I left the village behind, that the way was now surrounded by brooding peaks. It was both easy and natural by now, this transition between warm and boisterous conviviality and silent, solitary contemplation. To be required at one moment to be receptive to all and sundry and then, with the dawning of another day, to be thrown back on just one's own resources was a fine stretching exercise for a stagnant soul!

After the hard work of yesterday, today's walk promised to be a mere dawdle. In the hamlet where I had hoped to have breakfast, however, no one was stirring, nor was there any sign of a bar, not even the usual telltale crate of empty bottles. The only sign of life was a large snarling dog.

"*¡Hola, peregrino! Espera. Y tu, bruto, ¡cállate!*"

The voice had come from an upstairs window. I stayed where I was and the dog obediently fell silent. The door of the house was almost immediately thrown open by a woman still in her dressing gown.

"Come in. The bar's in the back. I wasn't expecting anyone so early. How did you find your way?"

"I've been walking for a month now. I no longer know how I find my way."

"*¡Vaya! Un filósofo.*"

She started up the coffee machine, and the first cup of the day was soon filling. There was also a machine for squeezing oranges, and it would be no trouble, the woman assured me, to fry some eggs.

"*¿Alemán?*" she inquired.

"*Escocés.*"

"*Ah, Escocia. Espera.*"

She rummaged around in a drawer until she found a calendar, a now much faded *Scotsman* calendar that a Scottish pilgrim had once sent to her. Scotland and Galicia, she had since found out, had much in common, each having a population of some five million souls, with Scotland having more sheep than people, and Galicia, more cows.

"And there are bagpipes here," she continued, "just as in Scotland. You Scots are always complaining about England, and we Gallegos, about Madrid."

The *albergue* in Tricastela was at the entrance to the town, and only a short way off the path. Park's *credencial*, I discovered, had already been delivered and would be waiting for him at the desk. I was also told that the priest of the village was a great friend to pilgrims and would be saying a special mass for us that night in the parish church.

"He has even written a poem," the elderly *hospitalera* added, "on the true meaning of the Camino."

"*¡Vaya!* A priest and a poet as well."

"And his poem has been translated into many languages."

There was a *ciber café* in the town, and I found a new message from Angelika. She said that she was well again, and she hoped to catch up with the rest of us by the time we reached Compostela.

"And you know what else? In the *albergue* last night I was given a room of my own, with no one snoring. For once I woke up smiling."

The parish church was situated just where the town ended and a field of beans began. The priest, who was a great friend of pilgrims, cornered me as soon as I entered the church, as he had done several others, amongst them Giovanni. Giovanni would read the lesson in Italian, I would read in English, and a Polish pilgrim in Polish.

I asked the priest about his poem. Yes, he said, it was true, his poem on the Camino had so far been translated into twenty-three languages, and most recently into Japanese, upon which I began to smell a rat.

"Just recently, you say?"

Only a few days before, said the priest, by a young Japanese pilgrim travelling by bicycle with his father. As the young man had no Spanish he had worked from the English version, claiming to be proficient in that tongue. Proficient in English, if I recalled rightly, to the point of having memorized a few set phrases which he offered in response to any questions put to him in that language.

Those of us chosen to read were seated on folding chairs behind the altar. I no longer felt any qualms about this, I even relished the opportunity, as if reading these once familiar lines in public, just as I might have read any other text, was, for me, a form of exorcism.

When the service was over and we had filed from the church, I found Giovanni and Sofia standing with Park. Lawrence called these three the Holy Trinity. Sofia rushed up to me and seized my hands in her own.

"That was beautiful, Roberto. I think that you must have been reading tonight from your heart. I almost started to cry. For the first time tonight, when you were reading, I was able to understand every word."

Beautiful perhaps, I said to myself, but hardly surprising that she should have understood the passage in English. The exact same passage had been read out just previously, twice, first in Spanish and then in Italian.

◆

What is more mysterious to us than ourselves? What is more in need of explanation? Why else do we feel the need, not just in adolescence but at various stages of our lives, to go in search of who we are? Just what is it that we wish to discover and why venture so far afield to conduct the search? Where, if not within us, could the self be lodged, and how could it possibly have escaped?

The first identity, as self-consciousness evolved from consciousness, was in all likelihood a group or clan identity, perhaps linked to some totem animal, an imagined helper, as laid out in the myths of the tribe. The myths of the culture were from the beginning a guide, a template in the form of a narrative for the self-making of the individual, and so it has to a large extent remained.

The soul with which we begin, it seems reasonable to suppose, comes from the first, faint self-consciousness of a frightened child, and the self that we initially create, at the prompting of the soul, serves as a shield to be held up before the world. As the snail, the clam and the armadillo grow shells, so the human animal employs a similar artefact.

We select from the models to hand: the male self, the female self, the well or the low born self, the hunter, the healer, the nurturer. The self, in all but the most exceptional of cases, comes off the shelf, and it would have been expected, throughout all but our most recent history, to last a lifetime.

The missing coherence which we impose on a complex and recalcitrant world, we also impose on ourselves. As we dream, create art or compose a story, so too we cobble together an explanation for what we are, and for what we feel and fear. We expect, by turns, as we rub increasingly against the world, too much of this construct, and too little.

The self may well begin to crack or fray. What was perfectly adequate for the adolescent may no longer accommodate the adult. Events, encounters and mishaps challenge the self, and when the self behind which we present ourselves to others no longer elicits recognition or sympathy, but only puzzlement, then the time has come to think again, to revise, or repair, for where, if we have ceased to make ourselves clear, must the fault lie?

◆

Patricia too had risen early so we set off together from the refuge in search of the bar that we had been told would be open for breakfast. Light was indeed spilling out from a doorway, but inside the chairs were still turned up on the tables. On the bar was a slab of tortilla left over from the night before which the barman offered to heat up for us in the microwave.

Patricia began to speak of her own life in Canada. She had grown up in Toronto, had gone to the university there, where she now taught. She had met and married a man who taught in the same faculty as she did, and who also wrote poetry.

"We're Paul and Pat to our friends. It sounds almost preordained, doesn't it?"

Most of what she knew about the medieval world she had first come to know through books. It was only when preparing her thesis on Chaucer that she had travelled to Europe, including in her packed itinerary a visit to Canterbury.

"I was blown away. I went back home and finished my thesis, but I also realized that I would never be able to understand what Chaucer was mocking until I had been on a pilgrimage myself."

A van pulled up outside, and a woman came into the bar with a cardboard box full of freshly baked croissants, which in Spain came coated with a thin glaze of sugar. Other things, Patricia said, had intervened, such as the birth of her children, but a recent seminar on Chaucer had given her the idea of resurrecting her thesis, fleshing it out, and turning it into a book.

"My husband says that I'm dreaming, that you can't go back to the Middle Ages again, not in Europe anyway. The only authentic pilgrimage left, he says, is the one to Mecca."

If she had had more time, she would have begun her own pilgrimage in Paris. People in the past would have set out walking from their own doorsteps, which indeed would have been a much stronger experience than hopping from airport to airport in order to begin.

"Poor Paul," she added. "He doesn't fly, and he'll be feeling really abandoned by now. His idea of getting away from it all is a weekend in a cottage beside a lake."

There was formerly, not far from Tricastela, a limestone quarry where pilgrims were expected to stop. The endless stream of pilgrims had been too good an opportunity to be wasted. Stones from the quarry, carried on by the pilgrims, would later be fed into the many lime kilns of Compostela.

The morning was fine, and the countryside splendid. This was the one aspect of the Camino which her husband would have appreciated, Patricia remarked. He was a poet of places not of people, better at impressions than emotions, with a genuine gift for capturing the spirit of a landscape.

"He's Canadian to the core. He couldn't write a line of dialogue to save his life. He can barely speak one."

The first of my own three marriage, in the late sixties, had been to a Canadian. We had met in graduate school, in Edmonton, Alberta, in the winter, and we were married before the onset of the following winter.

"My first marriage," I summarized, "was disastrous, and the disaster was me."

We happened upon a small market. Folding tables had been set up for the day under the colonnades of a town square. We purchased some nuts and fruit, a loaf of bread, and a large cheese, all that was necessary for a picnic somewhere down the road.

My second attempt at marriage was with a Lebanese. We were together first in Mexico, then in Montreal, then in Lebanon, and finally, when Lebanon began to self-destruct, we decided to return to Montreal.

"I've heard that Lebanon's beautiful," said Patricia. "The sea, the mountains, Baalbek. All it lacks is peace."

"Beautiful yes, but peaceful no. Not with so many religions crammed into so small a space."

The *albergue* in Sarria had a roof terrace affording views in three directions over the town and the surrounding hills. There was a clothes line on the terrace and, before stretching out in the sun, I helped Maika, the lanky German student, to wring out a pair of jeans.

"I wonder if we'll see that old man again," she mused. "Do you remember him? The one with the whistle?"

"Yes, the tramp. He seems to have made the Camino his home."

"I think so. Angelika told me that he might be dangerous, but if we are truly pilgrims we should also feel pity for him."

"By all means feel pity for him, that's my advice, but keep your distance."

Having hung up her jeans, Maika sat down cross-legged on the tiled floor. She had brought along a German translation of a book by Terry Pratchett but she hadn't yet opened it, preferring to talk. She was a strong walker and had had no difficulty so far keeping pace with the rest of us, but she wasn't sure whether she had the proper psychology to be a pilgrim.

"Perhaps I am too shy. Even at home, I am a private person. My friends say that I am too much locked inside of myself."

She was very young yet, and there were few other young people walking the Camino so early in the year, when most would still be in school. In the summer, I suggested, she would have met more pilgrims her own age.

"Yes, of course. In summer, I believe, the Camino is more frivolous. But I must not, I think, allow myself any excuses."

A bell began chiming the hour in the adjacent church tower. We had to wait for it to stop before we could continue the conversation, but Maika had clearly not, in the meantime, lost her train of thought.

"I must be, I think, the way that I am in my heart. If you are not as people expect you to be, then pretending that you are will only make you look ridiculous."

◆

The essence of the psyche, it has been stated, is myth, and psychology is thus essentially mythology, the study of the stories of the soul, the stories which have crystallized into our conception of a self. We are all, throughout our lives, subject to an identity crisis, according to this view, because a single self, a single identity, is a delusion, the characteristic delusion of a monotheistic mind.

Our prolonged infancy is followed by the extended apprenticeship of youth, the period of our lives during which we seek to discover who we are and what on earth we are meant to be about. More compliantly than critically, we draw upon that store of received symbols, stories, and precedents which are our birthright and to some extent our destiny, for we are neither endlessly creative nor infinitely malleable, and to live within any human society entails, amongst other things, the perpetuation of the narratives of that society.

Would we be regarded as sane? Then we will strive in our self-narratives for consistency, for regularity, for a narrative consonant with the narratives already familiar to us. Our initial version of the world, which now includes ourselves, is inevitably the handiwork of a beginner, a novice, a newcomer, a true believer.

It is our very nature to shape our natures, and we begin with what is to hand. The narrative conventions of the culture are the models for our personal histories, for the telling of our lives. We must speak of ourselves if we are sane, or wish to seem so, in a way that others will be quick to recognize.

What is told of a life becomes, until the next telling, the contour of that life. With time, with maturity, with the growth of understanding, a more complex, more nuanced narrative may emerge, one whose telling may even be subversive.

Prolonged or agonized introspection is always likely to produce heresies. And every society, every state and system of belief is vulnerable to what may be the greatest heresy of all, which is the revelation that there are, and may forever be, any number of stories that we could tell about the world and still not exhaust the possibilities.

◆

Lebanon, in those first months, had promised much. In addition to the natural beauty of the land, its coastal hills still preserved the remnants of a myriad of ancient cultures. The land itself, thus layered with human meaning, had been a palimpsest.

We began walking in the hills in the evenings once the terrible heat of the day had subsided, picking up finely worked chips of flint which were once the teeth of primitive sickles. The more that we found, the more carefully we looked. From those barren hills, we could look inland to the foothills of the mountains, or, to the west, out over the Mediterranean.

"Why do I suspect," said Lawrence, "that this will all end in tears?"

"Don't spoil it," said Patricia. "Let him tell it in his own way."

That had been in the summer of 1973, in the lull before the next storm. Our first find of note turned out to be a knife, or rather the blade of a knife, a piece of flint some six inches in length and worked on both edges. The very next morning we took a taxi some twenty miles up the coast to Beirut and the archaeological museum.

The museum had nothing like it. There might possibly be a similar piece in Paris or Ankara, the curator told us, but not in Lebanon. He asked how we had come by the knife, to which my wife replied that we had been given it by a shepherd. Afterwards I asked her why she had lied.

"Basic instinct, *habibi*."

We would never have discovered the pot had we not first noticed a portion of the rim already protruding from the surface. Having freed it we could then see the jagged edges of additional segments in the bottom of the hole. The pot, clearly, would have been huge, and we couldn't help speculating on what it might contain. The hill was only a short walk from the village and the house in which my wife had grown up, but it would never have occurred to her or her brothers to go exploring in those dry, bare hills where only snakes lived.

"Only an infidel would have thought of it," she teased me.

She was an infidel herself. She and her family and the villagers were all Maronite Christians, while the surrounding villages, as well as the port of Sidon which we could see from the terrace of her house, were Muslim.

Lawrence's glass was empty. He caught the eye of a waiter and used sign language to order another round of beers. Try as we might, we had been unable to find anywhere in the town of Sarria prepared to serve us supper before nine o'clock.

"To a Lebanese, in any case," I continued, "outdoors means the patio of a restaurant."

Some days we freed only a few shards of the pot, some days a section so large and of such a weight that we had to carry it back to the house together, on a blanket. By sifting the dirt as we removed it, we recovered several small bronze utensils and what appeared to be a tiny goddess. The pot itself was in all likelihood Phoenician, our research revealed, and had probably been buried in the ground to serve as a granary.

Weeks passed before all the pieces had been dug up, drawn, numbered, and carried back to the house. In the evenings, as we sat on the veranda painstakingly cleaning and gluing the pieces back together, we could hear the sound of distant shelling. The Arabs and the Israelis were by this time at war again on the Golan Heights and elsewhere.

Nevertheless we soon had before us a Phoenician pot nearly five feet high and at its widest point some eight feet in circumference. The fighting soon enough went back into remission, with nothing having been resolved and with all of the old hatreds still smouldering. Lebanon, we were thus forced to admit, had turned out to be a mistake.

A farmer appeared one morning with a cart full of straw. The pot was laid carefully onto the straw and secured with ropes. It was to be a house-warming present for a cousin of my wife's. We ourselves were back in Montreal when the civil war broke out in Lebanon and we were told the end of the story only some time afterwards: the pot and the house of my wife's cousin had been destroyed by a mortar shell fired into the village off the back of a jeep.

"It seems incredible," Patricia said. "I got married in the Seventies, had my children, and wrote a book on Christine de Pisan."

"I stayed high during the Seventies," said Lawrence. "I don't think I missed much."

Something which neither of us could have identified seemed to have unravelled. We found it difficult, back in Montreal, at yet another new address, to agree on anything. In the streets of Beirut, we saw later on Canadian television, even the priests and the mullahs had taken to carrying Kalashnikovs.

MOUNTAIN OF JOY

✝

I fear you will never reach Mecca, O Nomad!
For you are on the road to Turkestan.

Saadi

The Hindu texts teach that the Hindu soul perceives the perfume of past lives. The ancient Greek soul was the aperture by means of which a human being was possessed by a god or inspired by a muse. The Christian soul, similarly, was for the early Christians the means by which the faithful might apprehend their Christian deity. The soul might by an analogous reasoning be posited as the appropriate locus for the mathematician's recognition of the elegance of an equation, the engineer's sudden discovery of a solution which has long eluded him, the poet's appreciation of a fine turn of phrase.

But beware, for a concept must not be mistaken for something of flesh and blood, nor does a sensibility necessarily correspond with a sense organ. The soul being a psychological, not a physical, reality, is not to be approached with a scalpel. The soul is, so far as we know, a human capacity, a function attendant to, and growing from, our unique awareness of the terms of our presence in the world.

Where the soul is concerned, there's no such thing as a free lunch. Be the soul that of a Hindu or a Greek, a Christian or a Muhammedan, a thinker, an empiricist, or a rhymer, what we "perceive" through the agency of the soul will be in accordance with what we have already prepared ourselves to perceive.

The earliest, and most successful, of the doctors to the soul of whom we know, was the shaman. The shaman treated the soul with words, myths, and cautionary tales, and thus the shaman, the healer par excellence of disorders of the soul, had first to become a master of metaphor, equally at home in the world as in the realm of the imaginary.

A disorder of the soul was one which resisted treatment by medicaments alone, defying the natural remedies of the forest or the tundra. A disorder of the soul, by virtue of its resistance to the everyday measures of the tribe, was also a social disorder, bespeaking the secret infringement of some custom or taboo. Whatever other symptoms the victim might exhibit, a disorder of the soul bespoke isolation, estrangement, shame.

The shaman worked in full view, employing the narratives of the tribe before a gathering of the tribe. In doctoring the individual, the shaman at the same time addressed his discourse to the group. The shaman sang, danced, smoked, invoked the spirits, until the matter became clear, and the victim's infringement was brought to light, for no treatment of a damaged soul would have been effective, according to this model, without a rapprochement.

◆

Park wanted to know as we walked out from Sarria whether, like him, I was feeling homesick. I said that I was not, as the landscape here with its rolling hills and patches of flowering gorse was just what I had become accustomed to back home in Scotland. The main difference was that, had I been still in Scotland, I would have been sitting all day in front of a computer.

"That's not what I meant, brother. There's nowhere on this earth that we can truly call our home."

"If so, then that's unfortunate. This earth is where we live."

"For now, brother. But the home that God has prepared for us is for all time."

"Perhaps. Is that really what you're counting on?"

We hadn't walked together much on the Camino, in part because it took him so long to pack in the mornings. This, moreover, would be our last opportunity, as the itinerary which Park had worked out for himself before leaving Korea required that he speed up his pace over the few remaining days in order to reach Santiago in time to make his return flight.

"I didn't mean, brother, that I was homesick just for Korea. I meant that I didn't come all this way just to walk through the countryside."

He was homesick, if that was the right word, for Santiago, a city on which he had never set eyes but for which it was clear that he held great hopes. It was not to pray for a miracle that he had come, however, for, as a surgeon, he believed he worked miracles every day with God's help.

"Sometimes I have doubts, brother. Not about God, but about the Church."

Sometimes the Church seemed to him to be lagging behind, but he had nevertheless expected that in Spain he would find that river of the faithful that he had read about, and that he would be carried along by it all the way to the cathedral steps. Park shrugged. He didn't want to say any more, but his meaning was clear: the Camino was something other than a river of the faithful, and his "homesickness" was for what it had lost.

After walking for a time in silence, I asked Park what had led him to become a Catholic in the first place. Had he, as a young medical student, begun to harbour doubts about the supposed wisdom of Confucius?

"No, brother, but Confucius was just a philosopher. His wisdom was an earthly wisdom, the wisdom of a day, but God's wisdom is for all time."

This was the most difficult parting so far. The Camino, it was said, finds you out, exposing your weaknesses, revealing your faults, uncovering your lies, but Park had from start to finish remained just the same, just as he had presented himself at the beginning. He had not even lost weight, nor was his rucksack noticeably smaller, although he did now walk somewhat more rapidly. He moved on that morning, with his huge *bordón* and his sweat-stained hat, a bulky figure all but filling the narrow track.

A reservoir now filled the valley where the ancient pilgrim town of Portomarín had once been situated, the town itself having first been dismantled, stone by stone, and reconstructed on the hill above. As I reached the bridge at the approach to the town, someone was already waving at me from the other bank, someone instantly recognizable by the shock of red hair.

She had been expecting me, as Park had passed not long before.

"He wouldn't stop," Sheila said, "not even for a beer. I think he thinks that I'm some sort of witch."

She had been in residence for several days already in Portomarín, sampling the energy and the restaurants and sketching the pilgrims who passed through the *albergue*. This last was one of the new, purpose-built refuges recently built in Galicia and it was all but totally automated. The lights went off automatically at a predetermined hour, and would not come on again until the morning.

The restaurant to which she guided me was part of a row of older buildings in the original town centre which had been relocated up the hill. To begin with, Sheila suggested *empanada Gallega*, a savoury pie of the region, usually filled with tuna, octopus, or bacon.

"And what else have your investigations revealed?" I inquired.

I myself, after a month, had become a better listener, or at any rate a more passive listener. A lake, Sheila proceeded to explain, having been filled slowly over time by rainwater, gave off very little energy, whereas a reservoir, having been created by blocking off naturally flowing water, soon accumulated a great store of energy. This energy, however, was highly volatile and difficult to work with.

We compared notes on various other pilgrims whom we had both encountered along the way. I was curious as to what she made of Petra, the schoolteacher from Germany whose laughter had so captivated me.

"So she was your type, was she? In that case you got off lightly."

I too had heard the stories of people meeting on the Camino, returning home to divorce their spouses, and afterwards trying to make a go of it together in Spain. The reason, Sheila claimed, was that people walking the Camino built up a great charge of energy without even realizing it.

"It's nothing miraculous," she argued. "You can build up static electricity simply by walking across a carpet."

Who was attracted to whom remained a mystery, but in energy terms, according to Sheila, the process was perfectly clear. Energy itself had no gender, it simply energized, but once that had taken place and the sexual dynamic kicked in – zap! Gateways were opened, and previously clogged channels were unblocked.

As stories went, this one was surprisingly comprehensive.

"So you draw on physics, Freud, tantra, and what else?"

"Knowledge is never all in one place. Physics, Freud, Jung, tantra, feng shui, plate tectonics, you name it. The wider you cast your net, the bigger the catch."

An energy worker could usually determine within minutes just where the problem lay, just where the energy which should have coursed freely through a body, had become trapped. Energy should flow through the body in a similar way to blood, but just like the arteries the energy conduits could become congested.

"It's particularly noticeable in addicts," Sheila said, "or in people with other fixed ways of behaving. A transfusion of energy, in such cases, can bring about quite sudden and dramatic changes."

Some individuals were gifted with more capacity for channelling energy than others, but it had proved possible, through training, to increase that capacity. Those who began with a deficiency, in terms of the flow of energy, might not only learn to free up themselves, but would also possess an instinctive empathy with other sufferers. They would also have the experience and discernment necessary to spot malingerers.

Having worked our way through a huge platter of *asada*, delicious roast meat, and a small mountain of chips, we finished with *tarta de Santiago*, an almond-rich pastry decorated with a Saint James cross. Portomarín was famous for its own version of this cake, which was transported daily by small vans to bars, hotels, and restaurants throughout the entire province.

"And now," said Sheila, "I'll need to love you and leave you."

Her next destination, which she would reach by taxi, was a place called Ribadiso. It was in Ribadiso, during her first Camino, that she taken a particular liking to another pilgrim. This, she had come to realize in retrospect, had been her first, tentative lesbian experience.

She then took out another sketch from her carry-all. The drawing was of Lawrence, or of someone very much like him. A forlorn looking pilgrim was pictured sitting alone in a bar, bent forward over a half empty glass. The caption read:

> *Para quien no cambia de hábitos poco sirve el Camino.*
> Without a change of habits, the Camino serves for little.

"But now I really do need to motor," said Sheila.

◆

Disorders of the soul can be seen reflected in the crises of the self, which are its symptoms. The past is always being drawn into the present, and the very thing which grounds us, which situates us within a time and a tradition, is also what constricts and burdens us, and what may leave some plunged into despair. And as our cultures define for us our emotions, so too will a received taxonomy catalogue our suffering.

We may find ourselves trapped, hemmed in. At the heart of what it means to be human are dilemmas all but impossible to resolve. Craving absolute truth, we nevertheless cling to what is merely coherent and plausible. Our creativity is most often put to the creation of fantasies, and our precious rationality, in which we take such pride, is then deployed in their defence.

So our myths are destined to become dogma. What was born alive and fertile ends up set in stone and so becomes a handicap, an idol to be hauled through the streets on holy days on the backs of the faithful. Unhappy destiny, unhappy humankind! What is there, in the view of anyone not a part of the procession, to distinguish Corpus Christi from the Fourth of July?

◆

A heavy morning mist lay over the valley. The path out from Portomarín passed through forests and cultivated fields. There were rabbits about, the trees were thick with crows, and a farmer in the bar where I stopped for my first coffee of the day said that he had seen a wild boar that morning, just disappearing into the mist.

"If only I had had my gun with me," he lamented. "It's not the season, but I wouldn't have cared about the fine."

The day's walk from Portomarín to Palas do Rei was only twenty-six kilometres, little more than a stroll for a pilgrim with some seven hundred kilometres already in his legs. When I next stopped I wrote down in my notebook an exchange with Park which I had only just recalled. I had been describing Edinburgh, for long famed as a city of sceptics, as evidenced by the motto over the door of the Central Library: "**Let there be light**."

"God is light," Park had replied without pause.

The town of Palas do Rei was of no great size, but I arrived to find it clogged with traffic. The *hospitalera* in the municipal refuge was apologetic about the traffic, which the town, she claimed, could do nothing about. Most of what was on the move in Palas do Rei, pilgrims included, was merely passing through.

The only pilgrim to have turned up before me was Albert the Belgian.

"Yes," he said, "it has always been my habit to get up early and attend to my day's work while the day is still fresh. Also, as I am no longer getting lost, the stages have become shorter."

I staked out a bed and we then set out together to find a bar with a midday menu. The bar that we found featured a *comedor* with a panoramic view of the surrounding farmland, but as usual there were also two televisions blaring, one at either end of the dining room and both tuned to a news program reporting on the previous day's British elections.

A chart appeared on the two screens showing that the Labour government had been returned as expected, with a reduced majority.

"If I may ask," Albert said, "what is your opinion of British politics?"

About the same as my opinion of the *arroz con pollo*, the rice with chicken dish which we had just been served. We poked about in it with our forks, the only discernible traces of *pollo* being a bit of the skin and a few segments of the neck.

The largest of the marches in Scotland against British collaboration in the Iraq War had taken place in Glasgow. The streets of Glasgow that day were full of flags and banners, families with dogs and children, drummers, Quakers, nationalists, socialists, Greens, none of us, needless to say, mattering in the least when it came time for the decision to be made.

I made my way up to the church which overlooked Palas do Rei with my notebook. Already working there in the churchyard was Patricia, with her own notebook, crouched down examining a headstone. A cemetery for Patricia, a historian, was grist for her mill, just as each new pilgrim encountered was for mine.

A cemetery was a text of a special sort, Patricia remarked as I crouched down beside her, a text full of lacunae. There were dates, which historians loved, commonly accompanied by conventional expressions of grief, but the rest of the story was missing, obliterated, begging to be filled in.

The stone before which we were crouched commemorated the death of a child aged four.

"You can start from something like this," Patricia enthused, "and you never know where it will take you. The name of the child is French, so it might have been the child of a pilgrim."

"And if it were?"

"Who knows? Were the parents on their way to Santiago, or on their way back? Did they simply accept the death, or did they have hopes of a miracle? You see how each question leads on to another?"

While we were crouched down, I asked her to have a look at my ear.

The left earlobe had been painful now for several days, which I had at first blamed on my having been bitten there by an insect.

"No. It doesn't look like a bite. It's looks more like a blister."

Mystery solved. It was springtime, the sun was still in the south, we were constantly walking west, and my hat had no earflaps. The lobe hadn't been bitten, it was sunburned.

◆

Is it not practically a law of nature that to boast of attributes which we do not in fact possess will sooner or later result in our being found out? Why then, having invented a self, do we insist on it so stubbornly, even to the point at which that self, discredited in the eyes of others if not yet our own, may become but a mere caricature of what we sought to project?

According to an *exempla* appearing in the sermons of the Middle Ages, a woman planning to sin conceived the idea of first donning a mask, believing in this way that she might avoid the wrath of God. The sinful deed having been consummated and the mask having been removed, the woman discovered, to her horror, that she had succeeded in disguising neither herself nor the sin, for her face now bore no resemblance to the face which she had intended only temporarily to conceal, but had become imprinted with the features of the mask.

Who are we truly? A false face, any face other than the face with which we have been endowed by God or by nature, is a poor expedient. Thus the woman in the tale, far from covering up her weakness by means of a disguise, had in fact accomplished the very opposite: the weakness had become accentuated, the woman having succeeded only in exchanging what had been her true face for that of a harlot.

◆

There were those who happily breakfasted each morning in a bar, on *café con leche* and such *tapas* as remained from the night before, but the two Danes, Christina and her widowed mother, preferred tea, which they brewed for themselves each morning before leaving the refuge, and *magdalenas*, small fairy cakes which they bought each evening from a *supermercado*.

Christina was already in the refuge kitchen that morning in Palas do Rei, with her rucksack already packed and ready for another day's walk. I accepted her offer of a cup of tea and a *magdalena*, shrugging off the fact that all of the cups in the refuge were cracked.

"It can't be healthy," Christina commented, "but what can you do?"

Everything else was going well. Walking the Camino together was allowing her to become reacquainted with her mother after many years of seeing each other only at Christmas. Her mother's divorce and remarriage some years before, it seemed, had caused a split in the family.

"How could it be otherwise? My brother felt the same. Mother had brought a stranger into our midst."

The older woman came into the kitchen with her rucksack, smiling benignly. Mother and daughter exchanged a few words in Danish, which resulted in Christina's digging out and handing over their map.

"Would you mind my company?" she asked me. "Mother would prefer to walk at her own pace today."

It was she herself, Christina admitted once we had set out, who wanted to walk at her own pace, to stretch her legs a little. She was slim and fit, and it was all that I could do to keep up with her. She had first studied psychology, she informed me, and had worked for some years in a clinic in Denmark before deciding not to pursue it as a career. Instead she had returned to the university to study theology, and she was now a doctor of divinity.

"It was no great conversion, but something quite childish. The relationship that I had at the time suddenly turned sour, and that convinced me that I didn't, after all, know the first thing about psychology."

She had no particular axe to grind. She presented Christian theology to her students just as an anthropologist would have presented the beliefs of this or that jungle tribe, not as something to be proven or disproven, but as one specific way of interrogating the world.

"Have you read Kierkegaard? He's my best example. He struggled all of his life with the problem of belief. Even if you can't believe, I tell my students, you can still analyse."

When we stopped after a time for coffee, she insisted on paying, as she wanted to ask my advice. She had recently received an invitation to teach in the United States, but was in two minds whether or not to accept.

"I have the idea that religion and politics can get quite mixed up over there, and as you've probably already noticed, I'm not the sort of person to hold my tongue."

"You'll need to tread carefully then. If you're not for them, you're against them."

"And I suppose that that's the first question they'll ask me."

"The first question they'll ask is if you're seeking to overthrow the government by force."

Our next stop was at Ribadiso de Baixo, where the Camino crossed the River Iso, and where Christina had arranged to wait for her mother. As the day was hot, we sat down on the riverbank beneath some poplar trees, removed our boots and socks, and plunged our feet into the water.

"Why not go first for a holiday?" I suggested to Christina. "Go at your own expense. Set your own itinerary. Have a look around. For the most part the natives are friendly."

"I had a chance once to go to Chicago for a conference, but I got cold feet. I'm ashamed to say it, but I was afraid that I'd be swallowed alive."

"Forget the cities then. Go out west. One moment you'll be looking up at the Rocky Mountains and the next moment peering down into the Grand Canyon. And then there's Las Vegas."

"Yes, I know there's Las Vegas. You can go there, I believe, and see Venice."

Ribadiso was where Sheila had last been headed. Leaving Christina dozing on the riverbank, I called in at the *albergue*, where a young woman was sweeping the dormitory.

"A redhead? Of course I remember her. She arrived in a taxi, she had a good look around, and then she complained about the electricity."

"About the electricity or about the energy?"

"I suppose it might have been the energy."

A few kilometres up a steep hill and I was in the town of Arzúa. Already the refuge was nearly full of pilgrims, some asleep on their bunks, some on their way to the showers, or waiting to use the internet. The Camino Francés was joined here by yet another route, the Camino del Norte, producing another new influx of pilgrims, if not necessarily of the faithful.

◆

Shamans, saints, energy workers, faith healers, exorcists, mediums, diviners, a whole fantastic panoply of dabblers in the occult: is there any limit to what we can imagine? On the one hand how can we help but admire such ingenuity, and on the other hand ought we not to be asking ourselves, "Will we never learn?"

Much has yet to be explained. Much remains concealed from our telescopes and microscopes, from science's gaze, and what eludes our probes constitutes fertile ground for old wives' tales, for flights of fancy, for the workers of wonders. And yet somehow the world has moved on, astrology giving impetus to astronomy and the laboratory of the alchemist inspiring that of the chemist.

Philosophy meanwhile runs its own course, seeking to concentrate minds, and to bring us back to our senses when we have strayed too far. So, for example, the verdict of the philosopher George Santayana on what was not thought out, but merely pleasing to the ear: that he saw no possible objection to it apart from its being untrue.

Much has been done, but much remains to be unravelled. When all of the measurements have been made, and all of the available tests performed, a patient may still be asked by the examining physician, "And how are you in yourself?"

Well? Sad? Buoyant? Couldn't be better? Fatigued? Fed up? Just what is being asked after, and just what sort of answer is appropriate? Are we not in fact being asked, even if not in so many words, "And how are you in your soul?"

An intriguing question. A real Pandora's box of a question. How are we in ourselves? How are we in our souls? How long have you got, doc?

◆

Just two days now to go to Compostela, and something was wrong with my foot! Had I overdone it? Ought I have rested more? Had wear and tear finally caught up with me? Or might I not just have laced my boot too tightly? The muscle affected was at the bottom of my shin, and the swelling, redness, heat, and a burning pain were those typically associated with tendonitis.

It was another Sunday, and beyond Arzúa nothing was open. It was still possible for me to walk, but extremely difficult to walk without limping. The anti-inflammatory cream that I was carrying had little effect, nor did the tubular bandage around my ankle bring me any relief. My guidebook spoke of a rest area on the route, with picnic tables and a water spigot, but the spigot had, since the last revision of the guidebook, been labelled, "*No potable.*"

I was stretched out on one of the tables, dozing, when Lawrence appeared.

"Do you realize how many bars we've passed so far today? And every last one of them closed? This must be what Hell's like!"

Sometimes a story emerged all at once, in a flood, and it was as much as I could do to get it all down afterwards in my notes, whereas Lawrence's history had come out in dribs and drabs, over countless beers and *tintos*. The course of his life had been set in the Sixties when, as a long-haired misfit, he had left university with a degree in social work and a drug habit serious enough to prevent him, for most of the following decade, from holding down a regular job or keeping up a steady relationship.

A group of German pilgrims filed past us without slowing down.

"*Guten Tag*," one of them called out cheerfully.

"Which means, I believe," Lawrence pronounced, "as you Yanks would say, 'Have a good day.'"

If the Sixties had been a decade of relative tolerance, the Seventies had brought a backlash. He had supported himself with a series of menial jobs which, at best, had kept the wolf away from the door, and he had lived with a number of different women, but none for very long, and none so far as he could remember had been particularly sad to see the back of him. Eventually he had exchanged his dependency on drugs for a dependency on alcohol, and that was what had first drawn him to Spain, where alcohol was cheap.

I couldn't lie on that table forever. When I was off my feet the burning eased, but the first few steps afterwards were agony. As for Lawrence, one trip to Spain and he had become hooked on that as well, on the Camino, the various routes of which he had begun walking and re-walking between jobs or on his holidays.

We approached another town with a bar, but again, although there was a plastic bag containing freshly baked loaves of bread hanging on the front door, the Bar Milagro, the Miracle Bar, was still closed.

"That does it!" Lawrence declared. "That's the last straw. Never again."

Every visit to Spain had been the same, ending up with his swearing never to visit the country again, which explained, according to his own lights, why he had never made the necessary effort to learn Spanish.

Once upon a time, in the forest between Portomarín and Palas del Rey, the passing pilgrim would have been able to avail himself of an outdoor brothel. Men would be men. What could not be totally suppressed was thus carried out in a manner which would not put any reputable women at risk. Travelling on, the pilgrim would in a few days reach Lavamentula, now called Lavacolla, the last village he would pass before arriving in

Compostela.   Lavamentula, loosely translated, meaning: "Wash Your Privates."

There was no refuge in the town, just a *hostal* of several stars and a bar which advertised *habitaciones*. The bar was packed, as a Formula One race was about to commence on the television. A young Spaniard from the north, Fernando Alonzo, was at that time just starting to make a name for himself.

"No," the woman behind the bar replied to my question, "we don't have special rates for pilgrims. Here everyone gets special rates."

The room was cheap enough, but it reeked of stale tobacco smoke. We opened the window as wide as it would go. An alternative would have been to continue on to the barracks-like refuge on Monte de Gozo, Mount Joy, from which the city of the saint and the spires of its cathedral could first be discerned. The Pope, the previous one, the pop-star Pope, when making his own visit to Santiago, had conducted an open-air mass there.

I felt at a loose end. There was no reason to walk any further that day, and to do so would have been foolish, but I found it impossible to sit still. I put on trainers and set out for a stroll around the village, seeing no other pilgrims apart from the Germans who had passed us earlier and who advised me that I should by no means stay in the bar that night as it was a dump.

"A dump?" Lawrence said when I reported this. "A dump is fine with me if it means no Germans."

We were the only ones taking an evening meal in the bar. A table was set for us in a corner of the room and the waitress rattled off what was still available from the *menú de día*. The food was dire, but it brought us one meal closer to Santiago, and we had only to turn our chairs towards the television afterwards in order to watch Barcelona, which was on the verge of clinching yet another title in the Spanish Liga, playing in a half-empty stadium against a team which had already been relegated.

EMBRACING THE SAINT

✝

Dreams are true while they last.

Tennyson

The persistence of myths in every tradition and in every culture bespeaks their effectiveness. Supernatural beings that have never existed and wondrous events which have never occurred have nevertheless served marvellously well for the purpose of organizing human communities and coordinating their actions. The myths of the tribe, repeatedly reinforced by the rituals of the tribe, both shape the community and defend it, in the first instance against the threat which comes from within, against the corrosive and divisive power of individual human intellects.

Consciousness evolves slowly, fitfully, and unevenly, and those who fully understand the premises of their own culture are likely to be rare. Belief, in every culture, is the norm, and becomes problematic only in the presence of competing hypotheses.

There's no such thing as a free country, as every country has borders, and what exists to defend the community against chaos and chance, does so at a price. Alternatives are ignored, and possibilities limited. A degree of self-deception, culturally induced, lulls even the more adventurous thinkers of the community into right-thinking, and so lures them into complicity.

What encloses also excludes. Cultures erect boundaries which rule out whatever does not lie within those bounds. Taboos become commandments, commandments become laws. Only the deranged mind, culture would have us believe, fails to respond to the familiar cadences of the narratives by which it was formed.

And where has this taken us? Are we any the less anxious, any the less fearful? Are we able to distinguish the dangers which truly threaten us from those which we are invited to imagine? Are we genuinely capable of thought, of thinking beyond what has already been thought for us? Are we able to choose beyond the choices with which we are presented?

Little is new under the sun. What once worked, by and large, still works. Myths are retold, rites are repeated, fireworks light up the sky. The myths of the tribe find new life in the myths of the state, processions are re-experienced as parades, and wherever in the world age-old traditions may be lacking, you can safely bet that they will be duly concocted.

◆

Not having heard Lawrence come in the night before, I took care not to wake him. Getting up and dressing in the dark was all but second nature by now, and it was only when I had hauled my things out into the corridor that I found the note which he had left tucked into my rucksack.

Buen Camino, peregrino. Please pass on my regards to the saint.
I'll get there eventually but not, I think, at an early hour.
Peace and love, Lawrence.

Only ten kilometres now remained, just a few hours more of walking, and just as well. The burning pain which had begun in my instep was spreading and could be felt well up my shin.

That morning planes passed low over my head as the route now skirted the Santiago airport, running at times just outside its perimeter fence. It was a sobering thought that the distance that it had taken me a month to cover on foot could be flown over in little more time than it took to be served breakfast. What, on the other hand, would the airline passengers know of the hills below, of the rivers, villages or farmyards? What would they know of those with whom they had shared the journey?

A modern sculpture crowned the peak at Monte del Gozo. Three Spanish women who had joined the route in O Cebreiro asked me to pose with them for a photograph. They inquired after Park, remembering that he was a *coreano* and not a *chino*.

"We'll never forget him. He had such a friendly smile. He called us '*hermanas*.'"

For much of the history of the Camino, those approaching the city of the saint would be completing only the first half of their journey. However far they had already walked, just that much again would have remained before they once again set eyes on their home.

Those arriving at Monte del Gozo on horseback would have been expected to dismount and to continue on foot; those already on foot could show their respect by removing their boots and proceeding unshod. As only pavement and tarmac now remained to be negotiated, I was more than happy to exchange my own boots for trainers.

Amongst the numerous pitfalls of which the pilgrim was warned in the *Codex Calixtinus* were marauding Basques, poisonous rivers, unscrupulous innkeepers, beggars, shameless women, purveyors of counterfeit indulgences, and false priests contracting for masses which would never in fact be said. Pilgrims approaching the tomb of the saint were more than likely to be confronted by moneychangers, snake-charmers, musicians and dancers, and by a small army of touts who greeted the arriving pilgrims as if they were long lost relations.

The woman greeted me with a warm smile, as if we had indeed known each other all our lives. I must be exhausted, she sympathised, I must have experienced many hardships. If I wished to stay in a hotel, she could direct me to one, but she was also prepared, as I was clearly a *caballero*, to allow me, for a much better price, to stay in her own house.

Her "house" was in fact the second floor of a building only a few blocks from the cathedral. The rooms which she let to pilgrims were small, but clean. She kept no register of her guests, nor did she wish to see a passport, the rucksack on my back being sufficient to establish my identity as a pilgrim, she said, and to her all pilgrims were one pilgrim.

It was still early and there was not yet a queue outside the Pilgrim Office. I handed over my *credencial* for scrutiny, indicated my motive for the pilgrimage by selecting the box specifying "Spiritual and Other," and was handed my *compostela*, a document certifying the successful completion of the Camino by a pilgrim identified, on the document, in Latin.

The great square in front of the cathedral, the Praza del Obradoiro, was by the time I arrived already filling up with newly arrived pilgrims and curious tourists. I spotted Giovanni and Sofia, still wearing their rucksacks. They rushed over to embrace and congratulate me.

"Your life will never be the same after this," Sofia predicted. "Maybe you don't believe me now, Roberto, but wait and see."

"It's Robertuum now," I corrected her.

Just beside us, something was being explained to a band of Japanese tourists by a guide wearing a baseball cap and holding aloft a small flag. Some of them noticed us, and at once light bulbs began to flash.

"Never mind," said Giovanni. "Tourists know no better. Let them have their *fotos* and their trashy souvenirs, and the rest will be left for us."

The faith of someone setting off for Santiago de Compostela in an earlier age would surely have been confirmed by all that he found along the way in the stories of the Apostle, of the battles in which he fought as a champion against the Moors, and of the miracles which he worked for those who travelled to his shrine. Every stage completed, every hardship overcome, would have further strengthened the belief of the pilgrim by increasing his *need* to believe, as whoever, upon reaching Compostela, doubted that the remains of Saint James were buried there, would have made the pilgrimage in vain.

Albert the Belgian was still in just as much of a hurry as he had been on that first day outside Burgos. Coming past us on the stairs leading up to the cathedral entrance, he slowed just long enough to shake hands.

"Please forgive me if I go ahead. I must light a candle for my sister before the mass. Today would have been her birthday."

Pilgrims entered the cathedral through the medieval Pórtico de la Gloria, placed their hand on a hand-shaped indentation worn into its central column.   Some appeared bemused.   Surely this bordered on superstition, and idolatry.   Watching from above us was the saint himself, the peace-loving version of the saint, *Santiago Peregrino*.

Confession boxes lined the wall of the nave.   Clerics known in the past as *lenguajeros* were at times available to hear the confessions of foreign pilgrims in their own tongues.   So the first of the boxes was still labelled, in Latin, "**Pro Linguis Germanica et Hungarica.**"

The altar was resplendent in gold.   Those who so wished could ascend by a staircase above the altar and embrace from behind a gilded image of the saint.   The purported remains of the patron and protector of Spain were kept in a silver casket below the altar, in a small crypt. The sight of this casket would be, for those whose whole Camino depended on its contents, the true culmination of their pilgrimage, and its vindication.

◆

The cathedral itself is replete with stories.   A long history, with many vicissitudes along the way, has left it with many faces, many aspects, many layers.   An earlier structure on the site suffered damage when the city of Santiago was taken by the Moors in the tenth century, under Al Mansur Billah, Almanzor, whose name signified Victorious through God.   The relics were unharmed, the piety of one elderly monk being sufficient to protect them, but the bells were seized as a part of the booty of war.

The human voice alone, according to Islamic tradition, should summon the faithful to prayer.   In Córdoba, in the Great Mosque, the bells of Santiago were inverted, caged in bronze, and put to service as lamps. There was to be, however, a sequel to this history: with the eventual defeat of the Moors, the bells which Christian captives had been made to carry on their shoulders from Compostela to Córdoba were borne back on Moorish shoulders from Córdoba to Compostela.

From bells to lamps and back to bells again, and who can say if, even now, the story has taken its final turn?

The lifeblood of the cathedral and the city surrounding it was for centuries the ceaseless stream of pilgrims. Workers in silver and jet flourished, providing mementos for the pilgrims. Candle makers abounded, as candles in great numbers were required for the all-night vigils before the saint's tomb. Competing with the candle makers were the false candle makers who sold the pilgrims candles made from goat's fat rather than wax.

Pilgrims gathered in the cathedral by "nations," each one singing its own songs, and jockeying for position before the sacred tomb. There are records of conflicts having broken out, even of fatalities amongst the contentious nations. The temple of the Apostle, having thus been profaned, would then need to be "reconciled" by purging it with holy water, vinegar, and ashes before worship could be resumed.

Those pilgrims willing to surrender the worn clothing in which they had arrived were provided with a new set, and the old garments were hung on the roof upon the Cruz dos Farropos, the Cross of Rags. Pilgrims, the lifeblood of the Camino, were also an irritant. They contended and fought, they were filthy and smelly, and the burning of incense in the cathedral's great censer, the *botafumeiro*, would in the first instance have been for the purpose of fumigation.

◆

As we were taking our seats in the section intended for pilgrims, a woman suddenly stood up and confronted me. Her face seemed familiar, but I was at a loss to place it.

"What's wrong with you anyway?" she demanded. "Don't you remember me?"

The accent was familiar, as was the tone of voice. It was Rita, the Dutch woman with the injured knee whom I had last seen on the floor of the *albergue* in Tosantos, cocooned in her sleeping bag.

Having previously held back from hugging the saint, I hugged Rita instead.

"Congratulations. You've made it in good time. You must be feeling much better now."

She looked at me sourly, as if she were being accused of something dishonest.

"Not really," she replied.

The priest officiating at the pilgrim mass began by reading off the nationalities of those who had arrived that day, along with their points of departure. Included in the list, which would have been passed on by the Pilgrim Office, was a single pilgrim from Scotland, who had commenced his pilgrimage in Saint-Jean-Pied-de-Port.

"Robertuum," whispered Sofia affectionately.

At the conclusion of the mass, eight middle-aged men dressed in smocks appeared to swing the *botafumeiro*. Having first been lowered from the ceiling, the great censor was next lit before the altar, raised up by the *tiraboleiros* using ropes, and then sent arching high over the heads of those seated in the transepts, trailing smoke.

Casa Manolo was a restaurant well known to pilgrims. It was located only a few blocks from the cathedral, it presented its *menú de peregrino* in various languages, and the tables could be pushed together in order to accommodate pilgrim families of any size.

We first compared notes on where we were all staying. Giovanni and Sofia were in the *parador*, Patricia and Meika in a convent, the Danes in a hotel in the more modern quarter of the city. Albert, his mission having been accomplished, would be leaving that very evening to return to Belgium.

"Tomorrow I will be home, the next day I will be at work. I believe that it will be possible now to meet up from time to time with others who have walked the Camino."

It was only when this last meal had been completed and the *postre* dishes were being cleared away that the finality began to be felt. Notebooks and scraps of paper were produced. Email addresses were exchanged. We were all invited to come one day to Italy and to follow the route that Saint Francis would have taken from Assisi to Rome.

Most of the others intended to spend the remainder of the afternoon shopping. Patricia, however, who was scheduled to fly back to Toronto on the following day, wanted to visit the Pilgrim Museum, and she urged me to come along.

"You could help with the translations. You know what my Spanish is like. In return I'll let slip next term that your short stories are one of the best kept secrets in Canadian literature."

Pilgrimage, according to the definition on the wall in the Pilgrim Museum, was a ritual journey undertaken with the aim of achieving purification, perfection, or salvation. Bonds were established between a place in this world and a higher plane, as also between the individual traveller and a community. A personal transformation was initiated and effected through a series of rites that culminated in the moment of arrival and there, the goal attained, the pilgrim would be reborn.

"That's the party line," Patricia remarked. "The Church, of course, has always had to contend with the way that people actually behave."

We moved from room to room in search of what pertained more to pilgrims than to precepts. The paraphernalia of the early pilgrims was of special interest as so little of it had survived, few pilgrims having wanted to be parted from it afterwards. In their wills, many had specified that their staffs, gourds, and wallets were to be interred with them to accompany them on that their final pilgrimage.

We paused before a model showing how Santiago's cathedral had evolved over the centuries and how its architecture had reflected the changed times, until now we were left with something of a hotchpotch.

"It's a cliché by now," Patricia said, "that cathedrals were the encyclopaedias of their day. This one's more like a scrapbook."

She had been in Spain for little more than a week. She regretted, she said, not having had time to do more than dip a toe in the water, but she was way behind on her preparations for a course that she would be giving in summer school.

"I know, my husband is always telling me. I should be learning how to slow down at my age. But what if that turns out to be irreversible?"

Upon which, after a full-bodied pilgrim hug, she was off to hit some bookstores.

◆

For seven years the then Moorish city of Coimbra had been under siege before the besieging commander thought of praying to the Apostle for aid. Hearing of this, a Greek pilgrim keeping vigil at the shrine of the saint ridiculed the notion, referring to the Apostle as a mere fisherman. Just before dawn the pilgrim became aware of a presence before him, and realized that the saint himself had appeared, holding in his hands the keys to the city of Coimbra as a sign of its fall.

"*Caballero soy de Cristo*," the Apostle pronounced himself, "*ayudador de cristianos*."

The vision was prophetic, as news soon reached Compostela that the besieged city had indeed fallen to the Christians. Not only had Saint James, the self-proclaimed horseman of Christ and support of Christians, granted the foot-soldiers of Christ yet another victory over the hated Moor, but he had in the process of doing so also confounded a sceptic.

The twelfth century witnessed the advent of Archbishop Gelmírez, the uncrowned king of Santiago. His campaign of aggrandizement of the cathedral began with a tomb-raiding expedition to the sister city of Braga, from which he returned to Santiago to a hero's welcome, bearing the remains of a certain San Fructuoso. Many who first cheered the archbishop were nevertheless soon agitating against him, and the stranglehold over the city which the Church, through his agency, had assumed.

Gelmírez brooked no opposition. French at heart even more than Galician, in the words of Menéndez y Pelayo, and more a feudal lord than a custodian of the tomb of the Apostle, Gelmírez ploughed his clergy, in a trope of the day, with the share of discipline, becoming ever more, with time, a scourge of his own people.

Restless in his ambition, but clear of mind, the archbishop found himself in conflict not just with the Moorish enemy but with Christian kings and rival churchmen. Amidst these conflicts, surviving in times of chaos and confusion, Gelmírez succeeded in bringing to fruition works of great elegance and grandeur, and it was from this time, in the account of Torrente Ballester, that the cultural meridian of Europe could be said to pass through Santiago.

♦

It was disgraceful for one pilgrim to be drunk, the *Codex* warned, while another was thirsty. Wine imbibed immoderately, in any case, rendered a man oblivious, raging, idiotic, silly, insane, lustful, and given to sleep. The raucous singing which disturbed my sleep throughout the night, and which had continued until dawn, was not, however, the work of pilgrims, according to my landlady, but of university students celebrating the end of their term.

Rain was falling steadily when I left the house. Santiago was said to enjoy only thirty fine days a year, and that clearly wasn't to be one of them. Freed for the moment of both boots and rucksack, I began my day off by tracing the onward path of the Camino through the streets of the old quarter and out as far as the suburbs. A few pilgrims, unidentifiable under their hoods, were setting out in earnest, their heads bowed beneath the force of the rain.

I envied them, despite the rain. A few more days of walking, another ninety kilometres through the pine and eucalyptus forests, and one could end one's pilgrimage in Finisterra, or Fisterra in Gallego, gazing out at the Atlantic. Already the city of the saint had begun to wear on my nerves.

Back in the cathedral precinct that day's new pilgrims were starting to arrive. Some were limping. There were haggard faces. Many of the men now had beards, many of the women had given up wearing make-up. A famous sermon in the *Codex* spoke of the many poor pilgrims who afterwards returned home happy, of the afflicted who were made sound, of the wicked who would henceforth be considered to be righteous...

"¡Hombre!"

There was no mistaking this particular pilgrim, as he was protected from the elements not by a jacket engineered especially for the job, but by what little remained of the plastic sheeting with which the French pilgrim Yvette had provided him. He was soaked through as a result, and he had no qualms now about accepting my invitation to a cup of coffee.

Paolo cradled the glass of *café con leche* in his hands to warm them. It had been raining the last time that we had seen each other as well, he recalled, on the climb up to O Cebreiro.

"You were looking for a barn to sleep in," I prompted.

"And you were thinking of what you'd be having for your dinner."

He had been tired enough that day to sleep anywhere, and just as well. In the poor light he had mistaken a pile of straw, which animals had already slept in, for a pile of hay, and the stench had stayed with him for days afterwards.

"Cosas del Camino, Paolo."

"Cosas de la pobreza, Roberto."

Poverty, however, hadn't defeated him. Even after running out of money, he had refused to give up. Very shortly now his vow to the saint would have been kept, and what was more he had the address of a Portuguese priest living in the city with whom he was planning to stay. Not only was he counting on receiving three meals a day in the priest's house, he also had hopes of a bus ticket back to Lisbon.

"Here's how I look at it, Roberto. There can only be priests so long as people believe in God, isn't that so? And who would believe, if God did them no favours?"

The logic that followed was woolly, but then Paolo was still shivering despite the heat of the café. God, clearly, with so many people to look after, sometimes needed assistance, and that was why there were priests in the first place. Priests were stand-ins, they were there to take up the slack when God was otherwise occupied.

"So I get a few meals on the house, Roberto. As a result I keep my belief, and the priest keeps his job. Which one of us, then, gains the most?"

There was, in addition to thanking Saint James for restoring the health of his son, another matter which Paolo intended to take up with the Apostle while he was here. It was something which had been troubling him ever since adolescence, something which would not have been possible to discuss with a priest.

"Suppose that I notice a woman and I find myself attracted to her. Suppose that I try to get close to that woman, and she allows it. Then I should be happy, no?"

"That's been my experience, Paolo."

"But me, no. If I can have this woman, I say to myself, then why not one even better?"

Paolo took out his wallet, which was held closed by a rubber band. The wallet was fat, but not with banknotes. It was stuffed with photos, business cards, newspaper clippings, old lottery tickets as a reminder of which numbers not to bother playing again in the future, and postcards portraying various saints. He extracted one of photos and studied it himself for a moment or two before passing it across the table.

"This is my wife. Before she accepted me, I was crazy for her."

The snapshot was of a small, dark-haired woman, plainly dressed apart from the elegant shawl which she had no doubt taken great care in arranging just prior to being photographed. Paolo delved again into the wallet, producing a second photo, of a second small, dark-haired woman, this one posing on a beach in the skimpiest of bikinis.

"Then I got crazy for this one, even though she had other men before me."

So far as he knew, both women had remained faithful to him. His wife had given him three healthy children, his paramour only the one that was born weak and had nearly died. And now there was a third women, an employee in the bookstore beside the bar where he worked.

"I don't have her photo yet. She lives in a fancy house, with an old aunt who thinks that men like me are up to no good."

"So tell me, Paolo, so that I can put it in my notes. Will you going be back to your wife, the woman in the bikini, or the intellectual?"

"*Exactamente*. This is just my problem. *A ver qué dice el santo.*"

Let's see what the saint says.

EMBRACING THE SELF

✝

Quit, then, your meddling with heavenly concerns,
and take up your abode in yourselves.

Philo

Following the final defeat of the Moors and their expulsion from Spain, the history of the Galician Apostle becomes more and more the history of his cult. With no more battles to be fought at home, the warrior saint appears to have emigrated to the New World, along with countless Galicians before and since, where the battle cry of "*¡Santiago y a ellos!*" would for some time yet still be heard, and where cities newly rising from the jungle would eventually come to bear his name.

In Spain new enemies had meanwhile appeared, so it was decided to remove the relics of the saint from their resting place and secure them elsewhere in order to prevent their capture by the English pirate Sir Francis Drake. Before long it was even being proposed that a woman, the recently deceased nun Teresa de Jesús, Teresa of Avila, should be recognized as co-patron of Spain. A woman she might be, argued the reformers, but one with a known and universally recognized burial site.

Much was at stake and feelings ran high. Among those rising to the Apostle's defence was the dramatist Francisco de Quevedo, who, in his *Su espada por Santiago*, asked if the prizes of the generals were now to be bestowed upon abbesses.

The traditionalists gained the day. Santiago was confirmed by Pope Urban VII, in 1630, as the sole Patrón de España. This would not protect the city of the Apostle from the army of Napoleon, to whom it fell in 1808, nor did it prevent the victorious soldiers from being billeted, for the duration of their occupation, in the cathedral cloisters.

◆

In our final emails I had agreed with Angelika on where and when we would meet up again. There was a view of the cathedral from the café, and I had newspaper with me to read in case she was late. In fact she had reached the city in plenty of time to go first to the Pilgrim Office, obtain her *compostela*, and get it laminated in the adjacent souvenir shop. She thus appeared on time, her freckled face framed by the hood of her still dripping poncho.

She handed me the *compostela* to admire. Only another pilgrim would know just how much it had taken to obtain such a document, or appreciate why such an effort was worthwhile. Having shed her poncho and rucksack, Angelika asked where I was staying, whether it was far, and if it was clean and warm, as she had no intention of putting up with any more hardships.

"No? But didn't you tell me once that the Camino wouldn't be what it was if it weren't for the hardships?"

"Well, Bob, what I think is, I have now had my share."

She had been promising herself that, like Giovanni and Sofia, she would stay in the *parador* when she got here, but she was now having second thoughts. Having resigned from her former job before setting off on the Camino, it was now starting to sink in that she had no sure future back in Switzerland.

"A couple run the place," I explained. "The wife goes off every morning to look for pilgrims while the husband puts on an apron and rubber gloves and does the cleaning."

"And please tell me what does a man know about cleanliness?"

The landlady had saved Angelika the one room that had a window. The room, once the price was taken into consideration, Angelika had to concede, would do. I left her to unpack, but she was soon knocking on my door to complain that she couldn't contact her mother on her mobile.

"The phone rings but no one answers. She knew that it was this day when I would arrive in Santiago. Will you answer if she calls back?"

Having had her shower and put on clean clothes, she reappeared in my room, sat down on the end of the bed, and began braiding her hair. Her mother had warned her on the day she left Switzerland that she was crazy and was only going to make a mess of her life. Perhaps her mother wasn't answering the phone, Angelika speculated, because she didn't want to admit that she had been wrong.

The mobile sounded its tune. Angelika snatched it up, looked to see who was calling, and vanished out the door clutching the device in both hands. And was the successful completion of the Camino then, in her mind, a sure guarantee that she would *not* mess up her life?

Torrente Ballester, in a work compiled in 1948, had the following "spiritual warning" for anyone entering the cathedral at Compostela. "If you don't believe in God, then make believe that you do. Otherwise the doors of your understanding would be shut, and you will be blind and deaf to just what it was that the grandeur of a cathedral had been meant to communicate."

We toured the cathedral in the afternoon, between masses. We entered as tourists, stepping around a Latin American woman who was sitting in the doorway, and had commenced trembling as we approached. As soon as we were past, the trembling ceased.

"So this is it," said Angelika, not very enthusiastically.

A few people were praying in the side chapels as we walked past. Almanzor, the conquering Moor, having ridden his horse into the cathedral, had carelessly allowed it to drink water from a baptismal font, upon which the unfortunate beast, it was claimed, had dropped down dead.

We dutifully circled the two transepts and the nave. Angelika's mother, we now knew, had gone out only briefly that morning, to do some shopping. She had invited a number of friends over but had then suddenly realized that there were no cakes or sweet wine in the house for celebrating her daughter's expected achievement.

Angelika, by this time, was famished, and it was fortunately a feast in Spain simply to walk through the streets. A young woman in a white smock stood in the doorway of a bakery offering us samples of *tarta de Santiago*. Live lobsters were on display in the window of the restaurants and a notice in the window of a bar gave the time when a live football match from the Bundesliga was due to be shown.

We strolled from restaurant to restaurant to compare their fare and prices.

"What are *percebes*?" Angelika wanted to know.

I consulted the small, worn dictionary that lived in a back pocket of my trousers.

"*Percebes* are goose barnacles."

"And what are 'goose barnacles?'"

"A good question."

Or we might try *berberechos*, which turned out to be cockles, or *navajas*, which were razor clams, or *chipirones*, tiny squid, or *salpicón*, a salad of pickled vegetables and diced octopus. To eat really well here was going to require a whole new vocabulary.

◆

The story of the cult of Santiago had many and various chapters, a number of which took the form of documents which historians have since judged to be not just inaccurate but in some cases deliberate forgeries. The cult was clearly falling into decline when, in the late sixteenth century, there was found, in a hillside cave overlooking the city of Granada, what would come to be called the "lead books."

The discovery could not have been more timely. A leaden box sealed with bitumen was unearthed on the hill called Sacromonte. It was said to contain a folded parchment purportedly written by two Moors present at the ancient battle of Clavijo, thereby confirming what many were coming to doubt with regard to the Apostle. News of the find was celebrated in Granada with music and dance and the planting of crosses. What arguments would remain to the sceptics in the face of such a "proof?"

Alas, the documents were easily shown to be bogus. The author, if he had indeed been present at the Battle of Clavijo, would have required a prophetic knowledge of the Castilian vernacular. For the faithful there was disappointment, for the Church, embarrassment. The parchments, having been discredited, were confiscated by Rome, and what would henceforth be ridiculed as the Granada forgeries were thus reburied, this time in the vaults of the Vatican.

◆

The best way to view the cathedral without being overwhelmed by its grandeur was from a distance, and there was no better viewpoint than the Alameda, the hilltop park which divided the ancient city from its present-day counterpart. By the evening of my second day in Santiago, the sky had cleared and a cluster of craft stalls had sprung up in the park. Angelika, who I knew to be vulnerable, bad-tempered, fragile, resilient, reliable, stubborn, and a good companion, was once more at her best.

Avoiding the joggers and the women walking their dogs, we found a bench and took out our respective notebooks. After a time the streetlights came on, and beyond, over the tiled roofs of the old quarter, the cathedral and its towers were now brightly illuminated against the darkening sky.

"Will you tell me something?" said Angelica. "For what reason did you make the Camino?"

"Spiritual and Other."

"Please answer seriously."

"I suppose because my life had become too comfortable. Everything, apart from my writing, was easier than I had wanted it to be. And you?"

"I think I was the same. I was not comfortable in my life, I was suffocating. My life made no sense to me."

A bell in one of the towers of the cathedral began to strike the hour. One of the bells had supposedly rung of its own accord at the moment of the miracle of the roasted chicken at Santo Domingo de la Calzada. Another story told of how a pilgrim was robbed of a fine cape in Villafranca del Bierzo but found it again when he reached Compostela, behind the main altar, draped over the shoulders of the figure of the Apostle.

"And should we believe such stories, Bob?"

"They're to chew on, not to swallow whole."

It was too soon to say if the Camino had helped me to get to the bottom of anything. Perhaps it had indeed been wrong to begin with any sort of agenda, perhaps better simply to have waited to see what would happen. Perhaps what the Camino afforded, regardless of any prior intention, was a means of getting to the bottom of oneself.

The opposite side of the hill overlooked the university, hotels and apartment blocks, a skyline which could just as easily have been that of any other Spanish city. And thus the line of graffiti that we encountered as we left the park, sprayed onto the side of a litter bin: "*La mierda de su perro es su mierda.*" The shit of your dog is your shit.

◆

And what if a single process does indeed account for everything? For the structure of our dreams, for the crafting of our myths, for the shaping of our first fledgling human identity? What then follows? What light is cast on our activities, our beliefs, our afflictions and our sporadic successes in healing what it is that afflicts us?

It has never been the business of dreams to present us with accurate representations of our surroundings. The narrative in which the dream immerses us is shaped not from precepts, but from images. A dream speaks to us from within, from some other part of ourselves, in a language which, while not our waking language, we nevertheless experience no difficulty whatsoever in comprehending.

However cavalier in its treatment of the facts of the world, the dream may nevertheless possess fictional coherence. A dream convinces us, in the absence of competing evidence, by offering a story which, when we dream, we find plausible. Certain dreams which are more vivid and frightening than the rest will have an afterlife when recounted in the daytime language of the tribe, the language of myth, a language intermediate between the imagery of a dream and the language of things observed.

Two things exist, the world and our interpretation of it, matter and metaphor. What we perceive of the world we necessarily perceive imperfectly, distorted by our very manner of ingesting the world, as our expectations persistently override our powers of perception.

We may have moved beyond mere consciousness, but by how much? Is there yet a factual account of the world, or of ourselves, upon which humankind as a whole could agree? Are we alert to metaphor? To myth? Are we able to recognize a dream for what it is at the moment of dreaming, or only upon awakening?

Ar-Razi, a Persian physician and philosopher of the nineth century, described the world about him employing the following metaphor. The world, he wrote, is one large hospital in which, by definition, the patients far outnumber the doctors.

◆

A steady rain was again falling when I set out the next morning, this time wearing my boots and once more laden with a rucksack. I splashed through puddles, anxious now that I was on the move to have done with the sounds and smells of traffic. The plan was that Angelika would follow at her own pace, arriving whenever she arrived at that evening's *albergue*.

Once I was beyond the city I had the trail completely to myself. The way entered a forest and it soon began to climb towards an *alto*, which a few days previously would scarcely have caused me to break stride, but it was no longer so. Even with padding on my leg and with my boot laced as loosely as possible, every step was now agony.

After a time I noticed another pilgrim coming up the hill behind me, walking easily and rapidly. Rather than be seen to be limping, I waited where I was for him to come past me. The Camino might, in the end, have found me out, but why show that to anyone else?

The man was blond, middle-aged, and well tanned by the sun.

"Hello," he greeted me. "How are you? Are you speaking English?"

His name was Peter and he was Swedish, and our meeting here, he thought, was quite a big coincidence. Since leaving Santiago, he had met only one other pilgrim, and that pilgrim had been English as well.

"Perhaps you know him? He told me that he walks the Camino every year, but he has now become quite fed up."

Who else could this have been, but Lawrence?

"I think he is perhaps," Peter added, "an English eccentric."

I waited on the spot, eating some dates, until the Swede had moved on. The identity into which I had slipped instinctively at the start and which I was reluctant to relinquish, was that of the outdoorsman, the seasoned walker who never got tired, who never got blisters, who asked nothing from others but upon whom others could always rely.

By the time I arrived at the *albergue*, on the outskirts of Negreira, Peter the Swede was already settled in. His washing was hanging on the fence, and he was organizing an evening meal for himself and whoever else should turn up. As on the previous day, the sky had eventually cleared, promising another pleasant evening.

The path that day had been rocky and wet, and only now could I shed my boots. The relief was so great that I agreed to walk back into town with Peter to shop. As he was a vegetarian, the menu which he had in mind was a large mixed salad followed by pasta with a ratatouille sauce.

"I have planned for twelve pilgrims," he declared, as we filled a bag with aubergines. "If any more arrive, there will be more pasta and less sauce."

Different histories, different viewpoints. From the age of eighteen, he had been a seaman, first an ordinary deckhand and later a cook, which had taught him the importance of planning ahead. The Camino, which like the rest of us he viewed through the lens of his own past experiences, was in fact not dissimilar, he averred, to a sea voyage.

"At sea you must never say I want this or I want that. You must accept what there is and be grateful. The same lesson that a sailor learns from the sea, a pilgrim to Santiago learns on land."

Angelika, Maika and the other pilgrims who arrived that afternoon were put to work in the galley. There were no proper utensils in the *albergue* so preparation of the vegetables was carried out with penknives.

Lawrence arrived in due course. His usual routine was to have a shower, a short rest, and a quiet drink or two before giving any thought to an evening meal. Finding that everyone else was already hard at work in the kitchen thus brought him up short.

"You really must excuse me," he mumbled, "if I leave you to it. It's been a long day, and old legs they do get weary."

"Nonsense," Peter pronounced. "Every person here feels weary. Every person here has had to walk the same road today as everyone else."

"Very well put," Lawrence replied without missing a beat, "but not every person here has had to do it with a hangover."

◆

It may simply be that the world of matter to which our intelligence is so lately come hasn't been given to us to know once and for all. The world may be of a far greater complexity than we are capable of imagining, and thus be destined to remain forever beyond the reach of our metaphors, eluding forever the nets of our narratives.

Our own world, the world of human cognizance, remains a work in progress in which we ourselves are the chief collaborators, the authors as well as the editors. We are inventive, ingenious, and imaginative, we are no longer slaves to our instincts or captives of the present. We are humankind, and we are above all engaged, and caught up in, that apparently most singular of human activities, the making and the revising of the stories which define our world and which constitute our lives.

Are we unique in assigning ourselves names? Do we alone of all earth's creatures construct these selves, these identities which we hold to be unique, and upon which we so insist? Are we the only individuals yet to have emerged from the herd, from the pack, from the flock, or are we only the most fanatical?

◆

The first thing that she was going to have to do when she returned to Switzerland was to look for another job. The meal having been completed and the washing up done, we were sitting on the lawn outside the refuge, and inevitably our thoughts were turned to what the future would now hold. Speaking mockingly of "real life" was not, we must all have secretly known, any defence against it.

Angelika, as usual, was sitting with her knees clutched to her chest.

"All last night I was asking myself, what job is best for me? The same job as before, in a new place, or will I be brave enough to begin again?"

The hotel in which she had previously worked was one of a large chain. Everything done for the guests had to be charged for, and every service provided had to generate more profit. The hotel staff, as a result, cared nothing about the guests, apart from about the ones who tipped well.

"Also the employees are always asking the managers for more money. Every person of them is thinking, 'Without me this hotel could not run for even one day.'"

Lawrence came out of the *albergue* whistling to himself and set off without a word back down the road to Negreira. Maika came out and sat down by herself with the Pratchett novel. She had felt trapped, Angelika explained, between those who ran the hotel and those over whom she herself had been placed in charge.

"One day some sheets could not be found. One of the maids said to me, 'Angelika, you are a worker just like us, why should you care if we steal a little?'"

As the sun dipped towards the horizon, a bank of clouds to the west was beginning to take on a fiery hue, and we could hear frogs croaking. Angelika had begun twisting the ring that she wore on her little finger in order to remove it.

"I bought this myself, Bob, for my birthday when I was twelve. I said to everyone, 'Look at this ring that my father gave me.'"

She knew wines, not just which wines were supposed to be good, but which ones lived up to their reputations. She also knew German, French, and English for dealing with the guests likely to turn up at a hotel and even a little Turkish for dealing with the staff. What she knew, on the other hand, like the expensive but tasteful clothing which she had to put on to go to work, was not *her*.

"Also I am not a chambermaid, and not from Turkey."

She had known little about the Camino before setting off, only that it led to a place called Santiago, a place a long way from Switzerland. Perhaps, to begin with, it had been foolish of her to quit her job, but what about now? She had told herself that she would walk all the way to Santiago, and now she had.

Almost immediately she had begun dreaming about her father. The first time he had been working in a field as she passed, another time he was a waiter in a bar, but on neither occasion had she been able to speak to him, because he understood only Spanish. Each time, what she had wanted to ask was why, after their chance meeting in the street, he had again broken off contact.

A deck of cards had been found. Laughter spilled out from the refuge. The light had gone from the sky, and the colour faded from the clouds. Her dreams about her father, I said to Angelika, were uncannily similar to one which I myself had had some years before about my own father.

"Then of course you must tell me."

It had been just before my father died. I had not laid eyes on him for some years, as we lived on opposite sides of the Atlantic. In the dream I was walking alone somewhere in the countryside and I came upon my father lying on his back beside the road, in the bottom of a ditch.

"Suddenly I wanted desperately to speak to him, to put my point of view. I wanted to make plain, once and for all, the nature of my grievances against him."

But for some reason this wasn't possible. Rage had welled up in my chest, but I was unable to vent it. What I wanted to say to him but had never been able to was threatening to suffocate me, and this was no doubt what finally woke me.

"A few days later the news reached me that he was dead. He had died alone, in a hospital ward. It was as if I had seen him, in the dream, already lying in his grave."

The timing had haunted me ever since. If I had acted at once, I might have been able to compare the exact time that my father had passed away with the approximate time of my dream, but I left it too long. In the end, the proximity of the dream to father's death had been just one of those inexplicable coincidences.

"Fathers," I said, sighing.

"Fathers," echoed Angelika.

THE END OF THE WORLD

✝

You've climbed to the top of a hundred foot pole;
now keep on going.

Dogon Zenji

And so, once upon a time, the way in and out of Galicia, a route used by shepherds with their flocks, by quarrymen with their carts, by mule-drivers, itinerant harvesters and vagabonds, was redefined as the Camino to Santiago de Compostela. Bridges were built and forests cleared; hospitals and cemeteries sprung up along the way, and a new sort of traveller appeared to tread the valleys and the hills.

John Bunyan, at the beginning of *The Pilgrim's Progress*, introduces this traveller to his readers, through the medium of a dream:

I saw a Man cloathed with Raggs, standing in a certain place, with
his face from his own House, a Book in his hand, and a great burden
upon his back. I looked and saw him open the Book, and Reade therein;
and as he Read, he wept and trembled, and not being able longer to
contain, he brake out with a lamentable cry; saying, *what shall I do?*

Many still walk in what will have, by the end of the journey, become rags. Some are far indeed from their homes and all walk burdened. Some have books from which they read, and others have books in which they write, and the lament of those who today cry out would very likely be, "*What shall I do next?*"

◆

This would most definitely be his final pilgrimage, Lawrence solemnly declared. The sun had yet to appear through the morning haze, but he was already perspiring, and constantly pausing to shift the rucksack on his back. The events of the night before in Negreira, according to Lawrence, had truly been the straw that brought the weary camel to its knees.

"At first the natives appeared quite friendly. We were getting on like billy-o until someone suddenly produced a bottle of the local firewater."

Instead of being left by his lonesome to drink his beer, he had subsequently found himself being encouraged to down glass after glass of *orujo*, for which, moreover, he was not being allowed to pay.

"That stuff must be dirt cheap. Anytime any of the locals came in for a drink, he ordered drinks all around."

One drink had led to another, and then another. As an Englishman, he had a reputation to uphold, however unenviable, and he had been determined to stand his ground. The upshot of it all was that he had left the bar somewhat the worst for wear and as a result there had been a bit of a stink afterwards at the refuge.

"That Swedish bloke was still awake, and he didn't want to let me in. I was forced to insist, which didn't go down well either. He as much as told me that I was bringing the Camino into disrepute."

I left Lawrence in the first bar of the day, sitting hunched over his second glass of *café con leche*. The route today was half again as long as yesterday's, and the pain in my foot not one whit less. The only remedy was to concentrate on the path ahead and those who in all likelihood had first walked it, the devout of a now vanished faith led by their Druid priests to the western ocean to worship the sun as sank to its daily death.

Someone appeared suddenly out of the eucalyptus forest through which I was passing, a man carrying an umbrella and a curved pruning implement. Having found out that I lived in Scotland, he rattled off everything that he knew of it, adding that it had been his lifelong ambition to travel to Scotland to shoot birds.

"Of course I am just a simple farmer. How rich would I need to be?"

"Nothing's cheap these days. It depends on how you choose to spend your money."

"Exactly! Once a man's children are old enough to defend themselves, he ought to begin thinking of himself."

We were now walking along a gravel road. The forest through which we were passing, he told me, was on land that had formerly been planted with grain. But then word had spread that there was more money, and less work, for those who planted eucalyptus.

"Unfortunately what one could do, all could do."

Now much of Galicia was covered with eucalyptus, and there were more trees than anyone could come up with a use for. So what people were saying today was that a better way still to make money, and with no work at all, was to allow a wind farm to be built on your land. And what was more not everyone could do this, because not everyone owned a hill.

"But you?" I asked the eucalyptus planter. "You own a hill?"

"Not yet, my friend, but there are still plenty of ignorant people around here who haven't heard what a hill's good for."

He asked me then what I had made of the saint when I was in Santiago. I started to describe the two contrasting images, Santiago Matamoros and Santiago Peregrino, but this wasn't what he was after. He wanted to know what favours I was expecting, what favours I had asked the saint for before hugging him.

The pilgrim refuge in the village of Olveiroa appeared to have not long since served as a stable. In the dormitory I found Peter already cleaned up and sitting on his bunk writing a letter to his wife.

"I was just telling her about our friend Lawrence. She thinks that all Englishmen are like the handsome English actors that she sees in films."

I reserved a bunk in the usual way, by laying out my sleeping bag, and then began delving in my rucksack for some clean clothes. Lawrence, according to Peter's version, had returned to the *albergue* the night before, muddy and bleeding, with a story about having been knocked down by a car.

"The fellow was obviously drunk. I think maybe he had hurt himself falling into a ditch. He is the sort of person, in my opinion, who makes things as difficult as he can for himself and also for others."

By the time I returned from the showers, Maika had arrived. She had been awakened by all the commotion the night before, she admitted, but she hadn't really minded.

"On the Camino," Maika added, "one should learn to be patient."

Peter didn't agree. The first lesson to be learned, whether on the Camino or aboard a ship, was to show consideration for those around you, and not make difficulties. People who did make difficulties, people like Lawrence, in Peter's opinion, shouldn't have been allowed to continue on the Camino.

Maika frowned. This stick of a girl, over the course of the Camino, had increasingly found her tongue. Peter, she pronounced quite firmly, was being far too harsh, and didn't sound very much like a pilgrim himself.

"Even on a ship," she argued, "it's not allowed, I think, to throw someone into the sea just because he makes difficulties."

◆

The pilgrim, simply by setting off, initiates a change, and even more important than what the pilgrim carries is what gets left behind. A change of scene and routine awaits the pilgrim, and much of what was hitherto the case ceases to be so. The pilgrim, in setting out, is set adrift.

El Camino mismo hace su trabajo. The work which the Camino itself is thought by some to accomplish is in fact just the structure which it provides. The changed circumstance with which the pilgrim is faced, at first confusing and disorienting, also brings about new stirrings, awakens what may have lain dormant, accommodates unaccustomed thoughts. New ways may appear for telling old stories.

The world of the Camino is clear-cut, and what it demands of the pilgrim, even if not simple, is nevertheless perfectly straightforward. One must balance responsibility for oneself with care for others.

Beware of the pilgrim, the ancient sources warned, who returns fatter than when he set off. There were always some who called themselves pilgrims dishonestly, thereby seeking to gain the trust of their fellows only in order to rob them, seeking the smaller gain, according to the sermons of the time, without ever realizing the much greater gain of which their own ill-considered actions had robbed them.

◆

Angelika had insisted that I wake her up so that we could leave together at first light. I shook her with some trepidation, recalling what her mood at that time of day had been in the past. On this occasion, however, the face which appeared in the opening of her sleeping bag bore a smile.

"Yes, I am smiling. Do you want to know why? Because this is my last day of misery."

We followed a farm track as it rose gently into the hills, walking for some time in silence, with only the crunch of our boots to disturb the morning's peace. We had been told that there would be a bar open just where the path crossed a main road, and so there was.

"So now I am starting to like Spain," Angelika observed. "Now that I will soon be leaving."

Inside the bar, the woman seated behind the counter was reading *La Voz de Galicia*. She told us that we should expect more rain before we reached the coast, and then agreed to fry us some ham and eggs.

"*Jamón York*," she specified.

"*Vale*."

The woman took down an apron from the wall, the identical blue-checked apron that every woman in every bar and every grocery store and every post office in the whole of rural Galicia appeared to possess. We started on the bread that had been set before us; Angelika, as was her wont, tore off bits of the soft interior to roll first into balls.

"Tell me," she asked, "what is your best memory of the Camino?"

"You," I said, "of course."

"For once please be serious."

El Camino es una droga, el Camino se engancha. The Camino is a drug, we had often heard it said, the Camino hooks you. I understood this now, I told Angelika. I understood the way in which it was true, and what it was that could bring about such an addiction. Never before had I lived life so intensely as I had on the Camino.

"That's my memory. That's what I'll take back and hang up on my wall. And you?"

Our breakfast was at this point placed before us, and along with it a small carafe of wine. *El desayuno del día.* The breakfast of the day.

"Ask me again later," said Angelika, digging in.

It was no mere shower that was waiting for us when we left the bar, it was a downpour blown straight in off the Atlantic. We walked with our hoods up and our heads bowed, trying to stop the rain from being driven into our faces by the fierce, howling wind. The path onwards was already a morass, and it was simply a matter now of putting one foot in front of the other with mule-like persistence.

And then it was over. The sky began to clear again from the west, and the sun which broke through what remained of the storm clouds hinted at summer. Having briefly vanished behind a wall, Angelika reappeared wearing shorts. Then, cresting a hill, we had our first glimpse of the sea, and before much longer we were descending, picking our way down a steep rock-strewn track into the seaside town of Cée.

There was no further need for our boots, which we strapped to the back of our rucksacks. It was only a short walk around the bay to the neighbouring town of Corcubión and the restaurant recommended in Angelika's guidebook. The dining room was built out over the water, which was sparkling in the sunlight.

This time we would try everything. The waiter went off with our order and returned to uncork a bottle of Albariño.

"And your best memory of the Camino?" I prompted Angelika.

"That night in Burgos with Martín and Marisol, do you remember? We were so happy all of us, all except Declan. He was sad because he had to go home to get married."

"That reminds me. What about your boyfriend back in Switzerland?"

"Maybe he will still be waiting. I told him, Bob, no more ultimatums."

We made short work of reducing the large platter heaped with shellfish to a platter heaped with just the shells. Angelika, midway through the meal, had signalled to the waiter for a second bottle of wine, which we sat over until it was empty. No more ultimatums, she repeated. The Camino, by teaching her not to give up, had also taught her not to give in.

The sun, outside, was dazzling. Angelika had a flight to catch on the following day, and her plan was to walk on the short distance to Finisterre, have a look around, and take the evening bus back to Santiago. We walked up through Corcubión together, as far as the *albergue* on top of the hill. I told her then, after a last hug, to be careful when walking on the road.

"Yes, maybe I am a little drunk, Bob, but I will tell you something. Our lives will be better because we have made this Camino, and also because we have known each other. This is anyway what I think."

"And it's what I think as well, Swiss girl."

◆

The pilgrim's progress is unlikely to have been purely physical. Weeks of walking will have at times produced boredom as well as fatigue; some will have struggled with the hills, some with loneliness; some will have found it difficult to sleep, some will never before have experienced being so overlooked by others.

And if we are, in ourselves, largely what we have proclaimed ourselves to be, how can any pilgrim fail to have, afterwards, a new way of telling that tale? Having been by turns uneasy, puzzled, doubtful, surprised and overjoyed, who will not have been stretched? Who will not, by this exercise, have been made aware of new possibilities?

The Camino is both a path and a procedure. While walking the path of the Camino the pilgrim also speaks, listens, ponders, takes stock, compares. Whether or not the pilgrim walks with others, a common purpose opens the door to co-operation and comradeship, creating the sort of solidarity which has, over the full course of human history, been the rule rather than the exception.

Some pilgrims talk too much, some drink too much, some simply give up. No one is any longer sentenced to the Camino. Some pilgrims are childish, some remain childish throughout. Some would prefer more rules, and some fewer, and some believe themselves uniquely qualified to lay down just what the rules should be.

Some seek miracles, and some deny them. Some are sceptical, some pig-headed, and some are eternally hopeful. Some walk with purpose, others only in search of the next distraction. With some exceptions, the young congregate with the young, and the old with the old.

Perhaps there are miracles worked on the Camino, and perhaps not. Perhaps miracles are worked, but not exclusively for those who seek them. Perhaps it depends on what you mean by a miracle.

◆

From the window of the dormitory of the *albergue* above Corcubión, it was possible to see all the way to the next bay and the distant lights of Finisterre, of Fisterra, beyond which there was only the sea. I got up in the dark, felt for my clothes, bundled up my sleeping bag for the final time, and checked beneath the bed with my torch to make sure that I wasn't leaving anything behind.

Peter and the *hospitalero* were already downstairs laying the table for breakfast. Peter was trying to explain to the *hospitalero*, in English, the ways in which his life aboard ship had prepared him for being a pilgrim.

"*¿Qué dice este tipo?*" the *hospitalero* asked me. What's this fellow on about?

Lawrence descended from the upper floor in stockinged feet to look for his boots. Someone had taken it upon themselves, he grumbled, to remove his boots from the dormitory sometime during the night.

"And why should just one person's boots not be on the boot rack?" Peter retorted.

Lawrence wasn't for sticking around to wait for breakfast, and I saw his point. We set off from the refuge together. We went back a long way in terms of the Camino, all the way back to Roncesvalles, and the monks, and the snow that we had ploughed through.

We had breakfast in a bar an hour later, and soon we were walking on a beach picking up scallop shells to take back as souvenirs. His apartment at home was already full of these shells, but perhaps a few more wouldn't hurt, Lawrence said, considering that this was to be his final Camino.

"And when do you usually change your mind?" I asked him.

"Usually about Christmas. Christmas in Manchester can really do your head in."

We agreed to meet for one last drink later, before he caught the afternoon bus back to Santiago. Lawrence then strolled off in the direction of the lighthouse and I went in the direction of the harbour, where a fleet of small fishing boats was bobbing at anchor, and where a woman in a straw hat was seated on the pier with a sketch pad open in her lap.

"Hello, old timer," said Sheila. "You look like shit."

"Do I? I didn't think that it showed."

"It does if you know what to look for."

She closed the pad, slipped it into her carry-all, and then asked if I had been into the sea yet. Here, on this long sliver of land, was where the last of the pilgrim rituals was meant to be performed.

Her favourite beach was a rocky one just across the peninsula from the town, and facing the Atlantic. We arrived to find it deserted. We undressed quickly, leaving our clothes in a heap on the shore while we waded out, cautiously, amongst the boulders, into the still frigid water.

We didn't, as the custom had once been, set fire to the clothes which we had removed, nor did we lose any time getting back into them.

The energy in and around Finisterre was immense, according to Sheila, owing in part to the constant pounding of the waves, and this would thus be the ideal place for her to set up shop, to establish a centre for energy work and the training of new practitioners.

"They won't let me build on the beach. Probably they think that I'm a nut case, but never mind. I can build on the dunes just as well."

We were headed back for the harbour, where there were restaurants. The crucial thing when channelling energy, according to Sheila, was never to block or obstruct it, whether intentionally or by accident.

"Sure you manipulate energy, but only by opening a way, not by closing a way off."

Energy flowed naturally from where it was abundant to where it was scarce, and the task of the energy worker was simply to facilitate this process. The metaphor here was of a mill which drew water from a stream, used the flow of the water to accomplish its work, and then returned the water undiminished to whence it had come.

◆

Dreams and the way that we tell them, myths and their elaborations, the relation of works of art to what inspired them, all suggest that what emerges from the deepest core of our being does do in many and various guises, and our interpretations are thus never complete and can never be definitive, but rather constitute second thoughts, rationalizations, expurgations.

We are humankind, and what we find lacking in the world we hasten to invent. We possess a tool which we have yet to master, and with this tool we have crafted phantasms, false fathers, beginnings, endings, commandments, hagiographies, holy wars, and *autos da fé*.

We write large and we write small, and seldom are we still. We create the world and we create ourselves, fashioning identities through the stories that we tell ourselves about ourselves, so as to appear in false face as what we wish to be, so as to appear each one of us unique.

◆

The Camino had become, in Lawrence's opinion, far too crowded. The space and the freedom which the Camino had once offered were now things of the past. Every refuge now had rules as to when you could come in, when you had to leave, and even where to leave your boots.

"Or maybe it's just me. Maybe I'm wearing out my welcome."

We agreed to keep in touch, and that we would have to do a walk together one day in Britain. A walk one day, maybe, we left it at that. And then just a slow wave out the window as the bus was pulling off.

Sheila had not been sitting idle. She showed me what she had drawn. A pilgrim whose features had yet to be delineated was standing waiting with a rucksack still on his back at a *parada*, a bus stop. The caption scribbled in at the bottom read: *El verdedero Camino empieza cuando llegas al final*. The true Camino began when you reached the end.

"So what's next?" I asked her.

"I've already looked at a few plots, but they're not cheap. I'll need to go back to Australia and get some money together."

It would mean convincing her partner to sell the Brisbane house which they had bought after divorcing their husbands. Her friend was unlikely to say no directly, Sheila thought, but she may well dig her heels in.

"I'll need time to wear her down. In case you're wondering, it's me who wears the pants in the family."

"I wasn't wondering. I'd already come to that conclusion."

"You don't say. Is it really so obvious?"

"It is if you know what to look for."

A breeze was getting up. We could hear it in the tinkling of the riggings of the moored boats. For supper that evening, Sheila suggested, there was a bar which was popular with the fishermen. A small place, simple and cheap, and it specialized in *revueltos de gambas*, shrimp-scrambled eggs.

EPILOGUE

✝

Caminante, son tus huellas el camino, y nada más;
caminante, no hay camino, se hace camino al andar.

Antonio Machado

However far he may have journeyed to reach Santiago, the pilgrim's trials were only half over, as he faced just as long a journey home. Possession of a *compostela*, however, would have entitled him to concessions such as warm water for washing, larger helping of food, and better wine.

There were thus two currents to the river of the faithful. Returning pilgrims passed on what they themselves had learned and so was the lore of the Camino transmitted to those for whom a guidebook would have been useless. What was passed on by word of mouth would also, gradually, have been transformed, elaborated, embellished, enhanced.

Some would have stopped short. Many a pilgrim had found in some town or village along the way a niche in which to settle, a plot of land that was uncultivated, an elderly artisan without a son, an inn tended by a young widow. Some heard opportunity knocking, some heard the siren's call.

◆

The cathedral at that hour of the morning appeared to be completely deserted. A door had been left unlocked to admit worshippers for the first mass of the day, which was already in progress in one of the chapels. Only when I approached the main altar did I notice an elderly woman in black sitting in the first row, utterly absorbed in her devotions. Why was she praying alone there, to whom, to God, to Saint James, to what end?

Some months before my mother's death, she told me that only her faith and her religion had enabled her to get through life. Not her family, or her children, not nature, music, or friends, only her religious belief had made her existence on this earth bearable. And no amount of argument, she assured me, would ever change what she knew to be true.

It was my sister who was with her at the end, and who told me afterwards that the greatest joy for our mother in her final days had been having Bible stories read aloud to her, the very stories which she herself would once have read to us as children.

"And don't you find that sad?" I recall asking.

"I find it reassuring," my sister said.

The Camino was at once a path, a space, and a field of play. The Camino had been for me a time out of time, an interlude, but there were no longer any faces familiar to me in the streets of the city of the Apostle, and what was more I was starting to see ghosts.

A Santiago, nunca se llega; sólo se va. Another paradox, paradoxes being perhaps the modern-day pilgrim's favourite form. One only goes to Santiago, one never arrives. I was not in 2005, nor am I yet today, able to vouch for the truth of this, I merely pass it on.

The bus from Santiago to the airport only took twenty minutes. I arrived in plenty of time to queue at the counter of the airline which would fly me back home. It would be springtime in Scotland by now. Gorse would be flowering on the hills, crocuses and daffodils would have replaced winter snowdrops, and it was time for this pilgrim to cultivate his garden.

SOURCES AND ACKNOWLEDGMENTS

The myths, legends, and miracle tales which have, over the centuries, become attached to the Camino have survived in literature in various versions. My criteria for which version to relate has been largely subjective and aesthetic. I have in most cases selected that version which, in my opinion, makes for the best story. Among the many works which I have consulted are the following:

Liber Sancti Jacobi ("Codex Calixtinus".) Traducción al castellano de A. Moralejo, C. Torres y J. Feo. Santiago de Compostela, 2004.

Arribas Briones, Pablo. *Pícaros y picaresca en el Camino de Santiago*. Burgos, 1999.

Carandell, Luis. *Ultreia*. Madrid, 2004.

Carré Alvarellos, Leandro. *Las leyendas tradicionales gallegas*. Madrid, 2004.

Coffey, Thomas F. (trans.) *The Miracles of Saint James*. New York, 1996.

Frey, Nancy Louise. *Pilgrim Stories*. Berkeley, 1998.

Kendrick, T. D. *Saint James in Spain*. London, 1960.

Márquez Villanueva, Francisco. *Santiago: trayectoria de un mito*. Barcelona, 2004.

Melczer, William (trans.) *The Pilgrim's Guide*. New York, 1993.

Rudolph, Conrad. *Pilgrimage to the End of the World*. Chicago, 2004.

Sánchez Drago, Fernando. *Historia mágica del Camino de Santiago*. Barcelona, 2004.

Torrente Ballester, Gonzalo. *Compostela y su ángel*. Madrid, 1998.

A catalogue of the volumes which have over the decades influenced my thinking on myth, storytelling, identity, and healing would be impossible by now to compile. Perhaps three writers whose works I have found particularly good to think with can stand for them all: Claude Lévi-Strauss, James Hillman, and William A. Christian Jr.

I am pleased to acknowledge the help which I received from my colleague in the Confraternity of Saint James, Alison Raju. Her advice at various stages in the preparation of this work has been invaluable, and her guide to the Camino Francés (*The Way of Saint James*, Cicerone, 2003) was my constant companion on the journey.

Page 55 This quotation is reproduced from *The Dehumanization of Art* by Ortega Y Gasset

Your turn to walk the Camino?

Make sure you have the right Camino Guide for the route of your choice!

Each guide is in full colour with:
• Overview route planner • Daily stage maps with optional routes
• Contour guides with elevations
• List of all pilgrim hostels and alternative accommodation •
Town plans showing location of hostels and hotels • Sun-Compass to aid orientation • Practical notes on preparation • Equipment checklist • Dictionary with basic pilgrim phrases (Francés only)
• Historical notes and places of special interest. In addition to the physical route there are pointers to the Mystical path with Inspirational quotations space for Personal reflections and a Self-Review questionnaire to help prepare for the inner journey. All this designed to fit easily into your pocket with the latest slimline guides measuring only 11.5 cm x 21 cm (4.5" x 8.25"). While the map books are even lighter, they only contain the daily stage maps, contour guides and town plans.

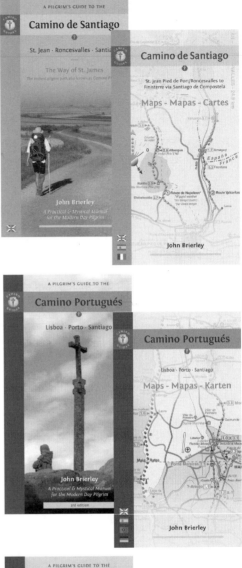